FACEBOOK®

Companion

FACEBOOK®

Companion

MATTHEW MILLER

WILEY

Wiley Publishing, Inc.

Facebook® Companion

Published by
Wiley Publishing, Inc.
10475 Crosspoint Boulevard
Indianapolis, IN 46256
www.wiley.com

Copyright © 2011 by Wiley Publishing, Inc., Indianapolis, Indiana

Published simultaneously in Canada

ISBN: 978-1-118-08700-8
ISBN: 978-1-118-13389-7 (ebk)
ISBN: 978-1-118-13391-0 (ebk)
ISBN: 978-1-118-13390-3 (ebk)

Manufactured in the United States of America

10 9 8 7 6 5 4 3 2 1

For general information on our other products and services please contact our Customer Care Department within the United States at (877) 762-2974, outside the United States at (317) 572-3993 or fax (317) 572-4002.

Wiley also publishes its books in a variety of electronic formats. Some content that appears in print may not be available in electronic books.

Library of Congress Control Number: 2011930021

My Savior, Jesus Christ, has blessed me with the technical and writing abilities needed to write this book and everything I have I owe to Him.

—Matthew (palmsolo) Miller

✛ ABOUT THE TECHNICAL EDITOR

TODD MEISTER has been working in the IT industry for over 15 years. He's been a technical editor on over 75 titles ranging from *SQL Server* to the *.NET Framework*. Besides technical editing titles he is the senior IT architect at Ball State University in Muncie, Indiana. He lives in central Indiana with his wife, Kimberly, and their four exceptional children.

╋ ABOUT THE AUTHOR

MATTHEW (PALMSOLO) MILLER began using mobile devices in 1997 and has been writing online for Geek.com and ZDNet since 2001. He is a professional engineer and naval architect in Seattle who served for 12 years in the U.S. Coast Guard after graduating from the USCG Academy in 1993.

Matthew began writing daily news posts and conducting reviews for Geek.com in 2001. He co-authored *Master Visually 2003* in 2004. In 2006, he launched *The Mobile Gadgeteer* technical blog (www.zdnet.com/blog/mobile-gadgeteer) on ZDNet and then expanded to his *Smartphone and Cell Phones* blog (www.zdnet.com/blog/cell-phones). He authored Wiley's *Windows Phone 7 Companion* book in late 2010. Matthew was one of the first 2,500 people to use Twitter; you can follow his tweets at www.twitter.com/palmsolo. He has been a Facebook user for years.

Matthew is also a husband to his beautiful wife of more than 18 years, Dayna, and a father to his three daughters, Danika, Maloree, and Kari. He enjoys playing and coaching sports, camping and vacationing with the family, and catching all the latest movies.

+ CREDITS

Executive Editor
Carol Long

Project Editor
Victoria Swider

Technical Editor
Todd Meister

Production Editor
Rebecca Anderson

Copy Editor
San Dee Phillips

Editorial Director
Robyn B. Siesky

Editorial Manager
Mary Beth Wakefield

Freelancer Editorial Manager
Rosemarie Graham

Marketing Manager
Ashley Zurcher

Production Manager
Tim Tate

**Vice President and
Executive Group Publisher**
Richard Swadley

**Vice President and Executive
Publisher**
Barry Pruett

Associate Publisher
Jim Minatel

Project Coordinator, Cover
Katie Crocker

Compositor
Maureen Forys,
Happenstance Type-O-Rama

Proofreader
Sheilah Ledwidge, Word One

Indexer
Johnna VanHoose Dinse

Cover Designer
Ryan Sneed

Cover Image
Ryan Sneed

✛ ACKNOWLEDGMENTS

I would like to thank my wife, Dayna, for her patience and understanding with my late nights and deadlines, and for helping keep me motivated to complete another book for Wiley. I thank my three amazing daughters for the encouragement and Facebook tips. I thank all my readers at ZDNet who visit my blogs on a regular basis and continue to make my daily writing about mobile devices an enjoyable second career. My friends Dieter Bohn and Kevin Michaluk helped provide screenshots for mobile phones I didn't have access to. I also want to thank my family and friends who were willing to be included in my book's screenshots.

I want to thank Carol Long from Wiley for working with me to find a subject for a book that I both love and enjoy writing about. My project editor at Wiley, Victoria Swider, was a joy to work with, and I can't express my pleasure enough in working with the fantastic people at Wiley again. Todd Meister did another excellent job in serving as my technical editor, and I appreciate all the editing services provided by San Dee Phillips. A strong editorial team really makes a difference in how a book turns out, and I think you will agree this Wiley team did a fantastic job.

✚ CONTENTS AT A GLANCE

＋ CONTENTS

＋ INTRODUCTION

Mark Zuckerberg is a talented computer programmer who started attending Harvard University in 2002. In January 2004, Zuckerberg began writing code for a new site and launched it in February 2004 as Thefacebook at
www.thefacebook.com. The site quickly grew in popularity and expanded from
Harvard to Stanford, Columbia, and Yale, followed by Boston University, MIT,
and others. The company dropped "The" from the name in early 2005 and
became known as just Facebook. Expansion moved to high school students,
then to specific company employees, and finally, in late 2006, it opened up
to anyone over 13 years old with a valid email address. Facebook reports there
are now more than 500 million active users with more than 250 million users
accessing Facebook from their mobile devices.

Facebook has become so popular and successful that a book about Facebook
by Ben Mezrich, *The Accidental Millionaires*, was adapted into a screenplay by
Aaron Sorkin and became the movie *The Social Network* in October 2010,
directed by David Fincher. As of mid-February 2011, *The Social Network* had gross
ticket sales of nearly $97 million. The movie won three Oscars for Film Editing,
Music (Original Score), and Writing (Original Screenplay).

Despite its popularity, many people are not aware of all that Facebook offers.
There is a huge and ever-expanding world of functions, features, applications,
plug-ins, and more associated with Facebook, and learning about these can
help make your Facebook experience richer and more complete. This handy,
approachable guide shares indispensible tips and shortcuts on everything from
sharing videos with a group to advertising for your business, and much more!
The compact trim size is perfect for taking it with you wherever you go, just
like you'll learn how to take Facebook everywhere on a mobile phone.

Unique to this Companion, you can find an extensive chapter devoted to
accessing and using Facebook from your mobile phone. With more than half
of the active users accessing Facebook on the go, you need to know what
your options are and what kind of experiences you can expect on the different
smartphone platforms available today. You will also find a chapter focused on

updated Groups features, a chapter discussing the December 2010-launched user interface, and a chapter devoted to the Places location-based sharing functionality in Facebook.

Face it: You need this book to enjoy your Facebook experience to the max!

CHAPTER ONE

WHY CHOOSE FACEBOOK AND HOW DO I GET STARTED?

In this chapter:

+ Why is Facebook the Best Social Network for Me?
+ Does It Cost Money to Join Facebook?
+ The Sign-Up Form
+ How Do I Associate a Mobile Phone with My Account?

Y ou may remember the days when you would call up a friend or family member, plan a visit, and then swing by to enjoy a meal and time on the couch checking out a photo album from the latest vacation. Or you may recall the days of trying to get your friends to all use the same instant messaging client so that you could chat about the latest gossip or movie you saw that week. These social interactions and many more have all changed with the introduction and adoption of Facebook. When Facebook launched in early 2004, you needed a Harvard-specific email account to join the network. It then expanded to other exclusive networks and finally opened up to full public access in September 2006 and currently has more than 500 million users. It is highly likely that at least one other person you know is a Facebook user. If you haven't signed up yet, it is time. If you have but you need direction, follow along to get started making the most of your account with this popular social networking service.

Why Is Facebook the Best Social Network for Me?

You may wonder what other competing social networks exist, and why you should choose Facebook. Several popular social networking sites are online other than Facebook, but each has a different main purpose and appeals to a different audience. The two biggest, aside from Facebook, are MySpace and LinkedIn.

+ **MySpace:** Launched in 2003, which, as of this writing hosts an esti-mated 100 million subscribers, pales in comparison to Facebook's 500 million plus.[1] MySpace was one of the first large social networks, but is much more customizable than Facebook and therefore appeals more to the creative mind, housing a large number of musicians, comedians, and fashion designers, whereas Facebook has a fairly standard look and feel.

+ **LinkedIn**: Launched in May 2003, this site has a reported user base of more than 90 million. It is targeted at business professionals and is com-monly used to make connections through employment history and to help people find jobs and employers find people to hire. It is much more about building up a network of associates, rather than Facebook's main purpose of sharing status updates and photos with friends. However, LinkedIn is adding more casual social networking features as well.

While MySpace houses the creative souls and LinkedIn fosters professional relationships, Facebook appeals to everyone across the board. Facebook not only has the capability to do all the things that these other aforementioned sites enable, but it is also socially accepted to do so on this social network. On Facebook you can post your artsy pictures, connect with your boss and colleagues, and game with friends on *Farmville* all in one. Facebook is for your daughter and your father; your business and your best friend. Facebook is for everyone.

Does It Cost Money to Join Facebook?

The short answer to this question is "No." It is free to sign up for an account and actively participate in Facebook for social networking purposes. There are two ways to spend money on Facebook, however: Facebook Credits and Facebook Ads. Neither is necessary to maintain an account.

+ **Facebook Credits:** In Chapter 12 (What Are Facebook Applications and How Can I Use Them?) you discover there is virtual money, called Facebook Credits, which are used in many games and apps. This virtual money does actually cost real money to purchase.

+ **Facebook Ads:** If you want to use Facebook for business or advertising purposes, you can purchase Facebook Ads, which are covered in Chapter 14 (How Can I Use Facebook to Build and Promote My Business?).

The Sign-Up Form

To set up your Facebook account, you need to simply fill out five fields and four drop-down boxes. Simply point your favorite web browser to www .facebook.com and the first thing you will see is the account sign-up/login form, as shown in Figure 1-1.

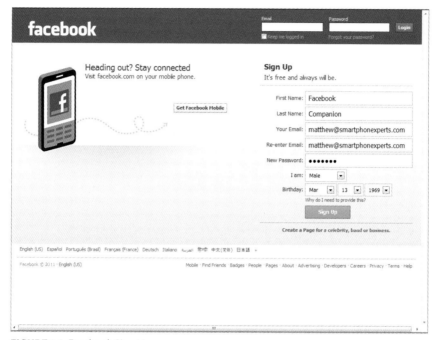

FIGURE 1-1 Facebook Sign Up page

Following are the only text fields that Facebook requires you to fill:

+ First name
+ Last name
+ Your email address
+ Reentry of your email address
+ Password for your account

CAN I CREATE MULTIPLE ACCOUNTS? Per the Facebook Terms of Use, you are not allowed to create and maintain multiple accounts. You can create a page if you want to share information outside of your personal profile. Pages are discussed in detail in Chapter 13 (What Are Facebook Pages and How Can I Set Them Up?).

Your password needs to be at least six characters in length; if you enter something shorter, a pop-up appears to help you resolve the issue.

WHAT CAN I DO IF I FORGET MY PASSWORD? Don't worry if you forget your password, you can click on the Forgot Your Password? hyperlink just under the Password Text field. You then need to identify your account with your email, phone number, Facebook username, or your name and a friend's name. Facebook then emails you directions to reset your password.

In addition to the five text fields you need to fill out, you need to use four drop-down boxes to provide the following demographic information:

+ Sex: male or female
+ Birthday month
+ Birthday day
+ Birthday year

As you can see in Figure 1-1, there is a hyperlink you can click to find out why you need to provide this information. The following explains why Facebook requires this information:

+ Gender helps Facebook describe you on the network. For example, it might state, "Add him as a friend" and want to know whether to say her or him.

+ A birthday is required because Facebook wants to encourage authenticity and provide only age-appropriate access to content. Per the Facebook privacy policy, you must be at least 13 years old to register for a Facebook account, and if it discovers that it has personal information for a child under 13, it deletes it immediately.

CAN I DELETE MY BIRTHDAY AND GENDER LATER? Facebook does not enable you to delete your date of birth or gender. You can, however, hide these fields in your profile so that only Facebook knows the information and it is not shared with your friends or the public.

By following these instructions, you are creating a personal Facebook account; if you want to create a Facebook profile for a celebrity, band, or business, you need to create a page first. Some people consider themselves celebrities, so if you are one of them, you may want to consider creating a Facebook page where all your fans can follow and interact with you. You can learn more about creating Facebook Pages in Chapter 13 (What Are Facebook Pages and How Can I Set Them Up?).

After filling out the five text fields and choosing values from the drop-down boxes discussed in detail earlier, click Sign Up and you are in.

Your account will then be created and the system will log you in. There are then three steps in the account setup wizard for you to follow. These steps are as follows:

1. Find friends using an email service (see Figure 1-2).

2. Provide basic profile information; high school, college, and employer (see Figure 1-3).

3. Upload or capture a profile picture (see Figure 1-4).

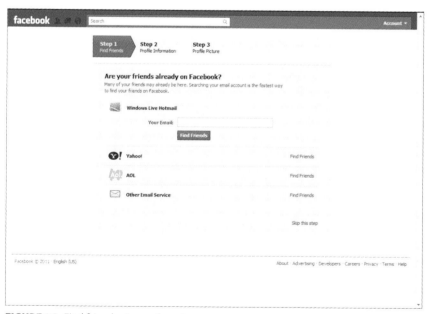

FIGURE 1-2 Find friends via email services.

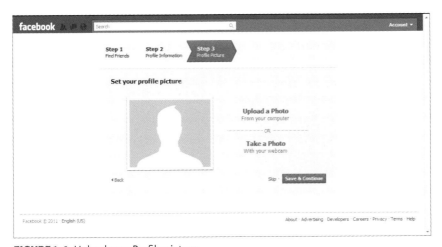

FIGURE 1-3 Provide some Profile information.

FIGURE 1-4 Upload your Profile picture.

CAN I SKIP THESE STEPS? Yes, you have the options to skip each of these steps if you want to set up your new Facebook account at a later time.

Because Facebook is commonly used to connect with old high school and college classmates, many women prefer to have their maiden name appear somewhere in their profile so that friends can find them more easily. Your account settings have an Alternate Name field; you can choose to add an alternate name right when you set up your account or add it months or years later, if say, you get married. Follow these steps to have your alternative name display:

1. From the Account drop-down menu at the top right of your Facebook page, select Account Settings.

2. On the line across from your name, click the word Change.

3. In the Alternate Name field, enter the name you want to add. (You can also change your name at this point if you recently married and are taking your spouse's surname.)

4. Under this field, check the box to have your alternate name also display with your account name. This lets people find it in your profile, friend requests, and search listings. If you enter a name and do not check the box, your name will still appear in search.

5. Click the Change Alternate Name button and your alternate name will be saved in your settings.

How Do I Associate a Mobile Phone with My Account?

As you can see on the left side of the Sign Up page or on the bottom left of the display, you can use Facebook on the go with your mobile phone. Click the Mobile link to see the four available options for connecting to Facebook on the go as shown in Figure 1-5. Chapter 9 (How Can I Use Facebook Effectively on My Mobile Phone?) covers a variety of ways you can connect to Facebook from your mobile phone.

Follow the specific steps in Chapter 9 to associate your mobile phone with your Facebook account; keep in mind that the Facebook Terms of Service states that you agree to update your mobile phone number in Facebook if you deactivate or change your mobile phone number so that a person who receives that number is not sent all your messages. This is also a safety precaution you want to take for yourself.

FIGURE 1-5 Mobile options

References

1. Harris, Andrew. "The Facebook bubble." *Business Spectator.* (www
    .businessspectator.com.au/bs.nsf/Article/Facebook-Myspace-
    Zuckerberg-Murdoch-pd20110304-EM86R?opendocument&src=rss)

Related Questions

+ How do I create a Page? **PAGE 201**
+ What are the different ways to get around Facebook now that I have an
  account? **PAGE 26**
+ How do I find new friends on Facebook? **PAGE 42**

CHAPTER TWO

HOW DO I SET UP MY PROFILE?

Your Profile is what defines you on Facebook and is the way you tell your story to your friends. The Profile serves as the database used to help people find you, initiate conversations with you, recommend apps to you, share common interests, and more, so you need to set up an accurate and descriptive profile to take part in the full Facebook experience.

You may think you already have a good understanding of your Profile, but Facebook is an ever-changing service, and this book covers details about the new Profile that came out in December 2010. The primary new feature is the way Facebook presents a summary of your profile at the top of your Profile page including your name, where you are from, where you went to school, other aspects of your life, and a thumbnail strip of you in recently tagged photos. This serves as an overview of you and gives your friends a quick visual of what is going on in your life.

Basic Information

Before you can make any changes to your profile, access the Profile settings area by following these steps:

1. Click on the word Profile in the upper right of your Facebook page. Your Profile page appears.

2. In the upper right below where you just clicked, you will find a button with the words Edit Profile. Click this button.

3. You will now be in the Profile editor with nine main sections listed as an index in the left hand side of the page. Click on Basic Information to access this first section, shown in Figure 2-1.

Aside from the required information stated in Chapter 1 (Why Choose Facebook and How Do I Get Started?), the information fields in this section are optional. Therefore you can choose which fields to complete—effectively controlling how much of your information is shown to the people you allow through the privacy settings. I recommend sharing as much information with friends as you are comfortable with to help improve the networking capabilities of the Facebook Profile system and to accentuate your own user experience.

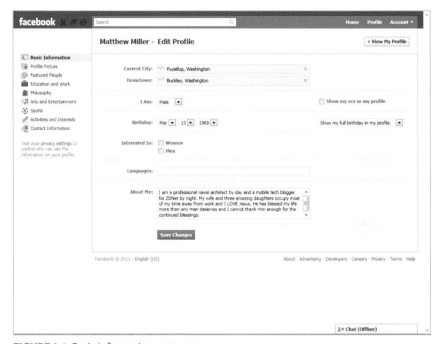

FIGURE 2-1 Basic Information entry page

CITY AND HOMETOWN

You can share two location fields with your friends: your current city and your hometown. The hometown is generally thought of as the place where you grew up and spent your childhood. It can be helpful for people trying to reach out and discover friends they had as kids.

WHAT IS THE MAP ICON NEXT TO MY HOMETOWN? After you enter a city name, Facebook attempts to automatically find it on Facebook with data provided from Wikipedia. You can find a map, description, demographics, and more when you click your hometown link in your profile.

GENDER AND BIRTHDAY

The Gender and Birthday fields were set up when you first signed up for Facebook, as detailed in Chapter 1, and cannot be removed. Facebook does give you preferences here though:

+ **Gender:** Here you have the option to make your gender (referred to as sex) visible or invisible in your profile.

+ **Birthday**: Here you can choose from one of the three following options.

    + Show My Full Birthday in My Profile.

    + Show Only Month and Day in My Profile.

    + Don't Show My Birthday in My Profile.

Facebook is well known for letting your friends know about your birthday by automatically noting in your profile summary that "Today is his/her birthday" which is fun to have out there for people to see and celebrate with you.

LANGUAGES

If you know any languages other than your own native tongue, you can list them in the Languages area of your Profile. This is another field that enables people with like interests and abilities to discover each other through the Friend Finder, discussed further in Chapter 4 (How Do I Find and Add Friends?).

- -

OTHER HUMOROUS LANGUAGE OPTIONS Facebook sometimes has a sense of humor, and it shows up under the Languages option. Under English (US) is an option for English (Upside Down) which, if selected, turns all the text on Facebook upside down for you to view. Additionally, after you have already chosen your language, if you scroll down to the bottom left of your Profile screen or home page and click the blue link that says English (US) (or whatever language you have chosen), a box pops up titled Select Your Language. Click the drop-down arrow next to English (US), and you have the option to try English (Pirate), which turns all your text into a humorous "pirate" take on all Facebook's terms. After you've had a good laugh, you can revert back to your original language the same way; just choose your desired language instead of English (Pirate).

- -

ABOUT ME

The About Me section is a simple text box where you can enter in anything you want that may not be covered elsewhere in your Profile. The About Me area is typically a catchall for things you want to share with people.

Selecting a Profile Picture

Your profile picture appears in a number of places and is what people associate with you on your Facebook account, so give some thought when choosing one. You can find your profile picture:

+ In the upper left of your own page

+ Next to any post or every status update you make that appears on other people's pages

+ Next to your phone number in your friends' smartphones (as detailed in Chapter 9 [How Can I Use Facebook Effectively on My Mobile Phone?], many phones now pull in your Facebook profile picture and assign that as the caller ID photo for you.)

Facebook gives you two options when adding a profile picture, as shown in Figure 2-2:

+ Choose a file and upload it from your computer.

+ Choose to take a picture using a computer-integrated webcam.

After you select a photo, you can also edit the thumbnail if the photo doesn't quite fit right. There is a 4MB limit to the size of the photo you upload.

You can change your profile picture any time, and it is good to update it often. You may also choose to embellish your profile picture with a *twibbon*. Twibbons are small banners applied across your profile picture and are commonly used to show support for a cause, charity, or other issue of interest. You can create one at http://twibbon.com/.

FIGURE 2-2 Profile Picture setup page

Setting Up Featured People

Back when Mark Zuckerberg created Facebook, one of the primary reasons for doing so was to allow people to connect with others to see who was in a relationship with whom so everyone knew who was eligible for dating. Today, a section exists in your profile where you can specify your relationship status and anniversary if applicable. You can also enter in family members and featured friends.

RELATIONSHIP STATUS AND ASSOCIATED PARTNER

Zuckerberg's original intent hasn't lost its significance; relationship status is something that many people do pay attention to.

The drop-down list for relationship status includes the following:

+ Single

+ In a Relationship

- Engaged
- Married
- It's Complicated
- In an Open Relationship
- Widowed
- Separated
- Divorced
- In a Civil Union
- In a Domestic Partnership

This field is optional, so you don't have to select anything if you prefer. Depending on the relationship status you select, you may see an option to link directly with someone else. For example, my relationship status states that I am married to my wife, and because we are both on Facebook, I have the option of linking my relationship status to her; in my profile you will find a hyperlink to my wife's Facebook page. You can also enter the name of the person you have a relationship with in the Text field even if he or she does not have a Facebook account. In this instance just a name appears with no hyperlink.

WHAT IS THE ANNIVERSARY DATE FOR? If you are in a dedicated relationship (married, partnership, and so on), you also have the option to enter your anniversary date and just like your birthday, your friends can be notified when your anniversary approaches.

If you change your relationship, you will see the notice that the previous relationship will be canceled or in some cases, the person you were in a relationship with before will be asked to confirm the change in relationship.

FAMILY MEMBERS

The section below your relationship status in the Featured People profile area enables you to list your family members who are on Facebook. I have a fairly tech-savvy family and therefore my wife, three daughters, brother, mother, and sister are all listed in my family section. A drop-down list for family member associations includes the following:

- Daughter
- Son
- Mother
- Father
- Sister
- Brother
- Uncle
- Aunt
- Niece
- Nephew
- Cousin (male)
- Cousin (female)
- Grandson
- Granddaughter
- Grandfather
- Grandmother

There is no way to enter in a custom relationship, such as stepfather or sister-in-law.

After you enter in family members, they will be sent a confirmation through Facebook so that these family relationships are verified.

FEATURED FRIENDS

You can also create lists of friends to make it easier to check in on those friends from your Profile page. For example, I have grouped my friends by college classmates, high school buddies, work associates, and close friends so I can quickly check on their Wall posts without having to scroll down all of my feeds to find the people I am most interested in at the time. Your friends appear in the left column on your Profile page, organized into your list groups. You can have friends on multiple lists as well.

Education and Work History

Similar to when you create a résumé, you can enter your employment history, college/university, and high school background into your profile, as shown in Figure 2-3. Facebook is one of the best ways to find fellow graduates and organize reunions, so entering in your educational history can help ensure you turn up on search results from fellow classmates and are contacted when alumni events are scheduled to occur.

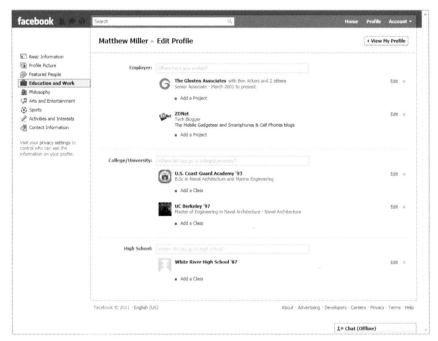

FIGURE 2-3 Education and Work entry page

Now take a look at how to enter in your high school data:

1. Click in the empty text box next to the words High School.

2. Start typing the name of your high school, and you should see the Facebook database auto filter as you enter your school name.

3. Select your school when it appears; you should see a couple more boxes.

4. Use the drop-down list to select the year you graduated. You can enter any people in your Friends list that graduated with you in the text box below the year.

5. Click Add School to save your high school entry.

If you attended college, you can fill out a similar form for the colleges you attended with the additional area for concentrations and majors. There is also an additional check box for college (aka undergraduate) or graduate school, along with a line to enter in your degree earned.

WHAT HAPPENS IF MY SCHOOL OR WORK IS NOT ON FACEBOOK? If there is no Facebook page for your school or employer you can still enter it and Facebook simply creates a hyperlink that goes to a blank Community page. If your employer or school is added later, you may want to update this information.

If your high school or college has a Facebook page, the auto-filtering mechanism should present that to you and when your educational institution appears in your profile, you can then click it and go to that institution's Facebook page.

Philosophy

You know how you were always told not to discuss religion and politics at formal events? Well, Facebook is not a formal event, and everything is fair game, so part of your profile is set up to enable you to share your philosophy with your friends. The Philosophy section includes places to state your religious and political views, list people who inspire you, and enter any favorite quotations you want to share.

+ **Religion**: You can use the drop-down list to select your religion or text box to enter a longer name. A huge number of options are available for you to choose from, so the drop-down list doesn't present all of them like some other fields; therefore simply start typing your religion and then select an entry as the auto-filtering mechanism goes to work trying to match your search term.

✤ **Political Views**: The Political Views section of your Facebook philosophy works the same as religion, so you simply start typing in your view and look for a word in the list that best describes your views.

✤ **People Who Inspire You**: Another area in the Philosophy section that you can use to help people understand where you are coming from is for you to list the people who inspire you. Again, you can start typing a name, and if a Facebook page for that person exists, it appears and enables you to select it. If there is no existing Facebook page, you can still enter the name. When you then go visit your profile, you see a hyperlink that can take you to a new page associated with that person's name.

✤ **Favorite Quotations**: Many people have favorite quotations and like to share them on their email signature, living room wall, or other place where the quotes are visible to serve as reminders. In Facebook you can use the Favorite Quotations section to enter quotes that define and inspire you, with the hope that they affect other people as well.

Arts and Entertainment

The Arts and Entertainment section contains open fields that can help you answer the following questions:

✤ What music do you like?

✤ What books do you like?

✤ What movies do you like?

✤ What TV shows do you like?

✤ What games do you like?

Thumbnail images appear for those selections you enter that have Facebook pages.

Sports

You can enter a list of the sports your play, your favorite teams, and your favorite athletes, as shown in Figure 2-4. Again, if any of these have official Facebook pages, you see their hyperlinks appear in your profile and you can select them as you enter their name in your Profile page.

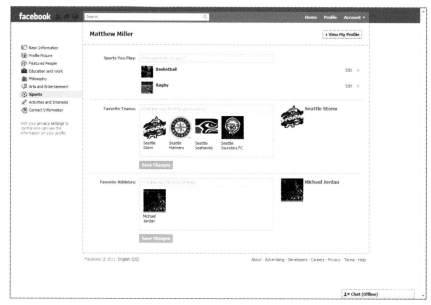

FIGURE 2-4 Sports entry page

Activities and Interests

In addition to sports and arts and entertainment, in the Activities and
Interests section, you list general interests and activities. Like nearly all these
Profile fields, you can leave these blank or fill them out to share with others.
Some of these activities and interests have Facebook pages associated with
them; similar to the Sports section, these are hyperlinked from your profile
with thumbnail icons for the pages.

Contact Information

Facebook is well integrated into several smartphones, described in detail in
Chapter 9 (How Can I Use Facebook Effectively on My Mobile Phone?), and for
many of us has become the means to keep our contact databases up to date
with the latest information. Therefore, the information you enter here may
be integrated into your friends' smartphones. Check your privacy settings

(see Chapter 8 [What Privacy Issues Should I be Concerned with and How Do I Set Them?]) before entering too many details into your contact information because you want to make sure you have full control over who gets access to your detailed contact information.

EMAIL

In the Email section, you entered an email address to set up your Facebook account, and you must maintain a valid email address to continue using Facebook. You can change this email address if you want, but if you make this request, you need to complete the verification process.

IM SCREEN NAMES

People often use third-party clients for chatting via instant messaging, and the IM Screen Names area enables you to share these with others in your Friends list. These IM screen names can be from the following services:

- AIM
- Google Talk
- Windows Live Messenger
- Skype
- Yahoo! Messenger
- Gadu-Gadu
- ICQ
- Twitter
- And several more worldwide

Remember: You can chat with others directly within the Facebook environment, so you may want to encourage others to join you there, unless they have specific needs for these other third-party clients.

PHONE NUMBERS

In the Phone Numbers area, you can add other phone numbers that you want to share with your friends to match a native contact database. You can use the pull-down lists to select work, home, or mobile phone numbers. You can have multiple numbers for mobile as well so that all your phones are covered.

ADDRESS

Your address is not used for anything in this Address section except for your contact information. You already entered your hometown and city you lived in on the Basic Information page described earlier in this chapter. Like your additional phone numbers, entering data here is designed so that others can store the information in their contact database.

WEBSITES

The last area for you to enter contact information into your profile is for websites you own, write for, or want to simply associate with your Facebook profile. After entering URLs for websites, when you view your profile, you find they are hyperlinks so that people can quickly visit your websites if you have them listed on your Profile page.

Related Questions

+ How do I set privacy controls on my information? **PAGE 109**

+ How do I find family members so that I can add them to my profile? **PAGE 42**

+ How can I join a group with similar interests? **PAGE 168**

CHAPTER THREE

HOW DO I NAVIGATE FACEBOOK?

acebook is a bit different than other social networking sites in the level of customization available for each Facebook page. All Facebook pages look the same in nearly every web browser so that the unique part of each person's Facebook page is not a busy banner or gaudy background, but in the information posted and the presented connections to different people. When you learn all about how Facebook pages are organized and laid out, you can easily navigate all of Facebook, until it decides to make changes to the user interface (UI) again.

Top Blue Bar

You have probably figured out some of the basics of navigation through Facebook simply by trial and error as you signed up and set up your profile. As you can see, the top blue bar area is the most important area to understand. Now work your way from left (see Figure 3-1) to right (see Figure 3-2) across the blue bar to understand each piece in more detail.

FIGURE 3-1 Top left of blue bar

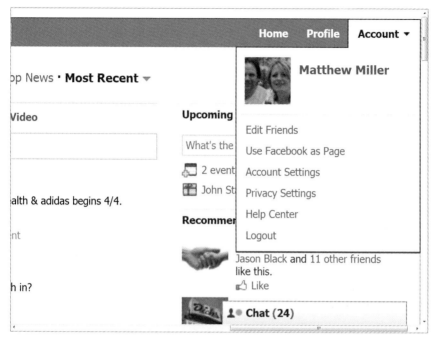

FIGURE 3-2 Top right of blue bar

See the following for the details on the blue bar from left to right.

+ **Facebook name:** Clicking this takes you to www.facebook.com and if you are logged in takes you back to your News Feed page with a single click.

+ **People icon:** Clicking this makes a pop-up appear listing any new friend requests you may have received. You can also click hyperlinks to see all friend requests (in case you ignored some and want to see them again) and a Find Friends link that launches the Friend Finder. See Chapter 4 (How Do I Find and Add Friends?) for more on how to use the Friend Finder.

+ **Conversation bubble icon:** Clicking this icon pops up your list of recent messages with links to see all messages and send a new message. Chapter 5 (How Do I Communicate With Friends?) covers Messages in detail.

+ **Globe icon:** Clicking this icon pops up a list of your recent notifications with the ability to click and see all your notifications. Notifications are covered later in this chapter.

✦ **Search box:** After placing your cursor in the search box, simply start entering text to see Facebook auto filter your friends, friends of friends, the entire Facebook database of people, apps, pages, and more. When you see what you are searching for, simply click on it to go to it. By default, the top eight search results are shown in the pop-up, but you can again click the hyperlink on the bottom to see more search results.

✦ **Home:** When you click the word Home, you return to your home page that shows your News Feed in the center and the rest of the page as you normally see it.

✦ **Profile:** When you click Profile, you go to your Profile page that shows your Profile Summary area (as described in Chapter 2 [How Do I Set Up My Profile?]), recent activity in the center area, and featured friends in the left column. You also see a button that enables you to edit your profile.

✦ **Find Friends:** If you do not yet have any Facebook friends then a link to find some will appear between Profile and Account. However, as soon as you have at least one friend, this option will disappear from your Facebook page.

✦ **Account:** When you click Account, a pop-up appears first with a link to your name and avatar that serves as a quick way to go to your Profile page. Below this you see hyperlinks to Edit Friends, use Facebook as Page (Chapter 13 [What are Facebook Pages and How Can I Set Them Up?] will discuss this option that you may or may not have in more detail), access Account Settings, access Privacy Settings, view the Help Center, and log out of Facebook.

- -

UNIVERSAL BLUE BAR Did you notice that the blue bar and all its functionality appear on all of your Facebook pages, even in the Help Center? Get to know the blue bar because you use it quite a bit and it's the quickest way to navigate around Facebook.

- -

You can click each result that shows up in the left of the bar for friend requests, messages, and notifications to see more details for that particular request, message, or notification.

Down the Left Side

The left column on your home page is useful for quick access to the main features of Facebook. The left column has four main sections, as shown in Figure 3-3. The first section contains your News Feed, Messages, Events, and Friends. The second shows your groups, the third your most used apps, and the final section is a rather new block that shows you small thumbnail pictures of friends online and available to chat with.

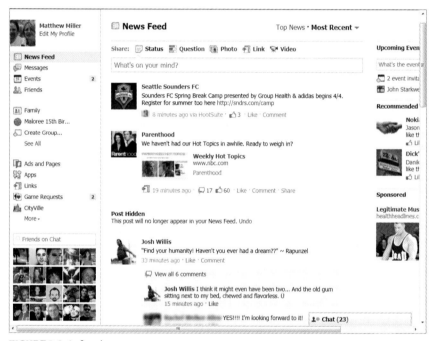

FIGURE 3-3 Left column

The top main block of the left column shows you current information with dynamic counters. This top block shows you the following:

✦ **News Feed:** Clicking this takes you back to your News Feed, which is the same result that happens when you click the word Home in the top-right area of the blue bar.

✦ **Messages:** Clicking this takes you to the Messages area where you can read and create private messages to your friends. These messages do not appear in your status updates nor do they require both parties (sender and recipient) to be online at the same time. You will also see submenu items for updates (messages sent to you as updates from pages you like and subscribe to), and Sent Messages appear in the left column when you click on Messages.

✦ **Events:** When you click Events, a submenu of items for friends' events, birthdays, and past events appears to help you filter your events. Also, by clicking this option the center panel of your Facebook page will contain event invites, upcoming events, a button to create an event, and more that will be covered in detail in Chapter 7 (What Are Events and How Can I Use Them?).

✦ **Friends:** A submenu for recently updated friends appears in the left column while the center of your Facebook page changes to show you ways to find friends and view or edit existing friends. Chapter 4 (How Do I Find and Add Friends?) covers finding and adding friends.

- -

DYNAMIC COUNTERS KEEP YOU INFORMED Small numbers in the left column appear when you have unread messages, pending events, and other open requests or notifications for the particular type of information listed.

- -

✦ **Create a Group:** In the next section you can view and manage groups. Groups are ways you can create collections of your friends for open, closed, or secret communications just within the group, which Chapter 5 (How Do I Communicate With Friends?) covers in more detail. Clicking groups in the left column changes your center column into the Group Communication area.

✦ **Apps:** The following section in the left column shows your frequently used apps, such as photos, game requests, notes, and more; this area changes for each person depending on their usage patterns. Notifications appear if the app supports it, such as for game requests.

✦ **Friends on Chat**: The final section of the left column is where you see your online friends available to chat when you too have your status set to online mode. If you look in the bottom-right corner, you can see if your friends are idle or available to chat. If you do not recognize their thumbnail, you can also choose to hover your mouse over their image and their name appears.

News Feed

The News Feed is the center column of your Facebook home page and is likely where you will spend quite a bit of time catching up on what your friends are doing. This area is a constantly updating list of status updates, photo tags, friend requests, shared links, event requests, group membership, and much more (see Figure 3-4).

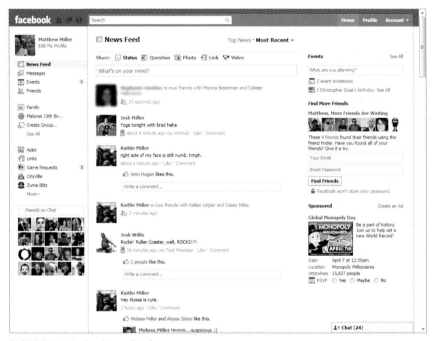

FIGURE 3-4 Active News Feed

The two filters at the top right by default are set to Top News and Most Recent. If you click the down arrow next to the Most Recent option, you see that you can change this to be one of the following:

+ Most Recent

+ Games

+ Status Updates

+ Photos

+ Links

+ Pages
+ Selected Group
+ Edit Options

WHAT MAKES THE TOP NEWS LIST? Facebook has an algorithm to generate your Top News based on things such as how many friends are commenting on the content, what type of content it is, and who posted the content. You will never actually know what makes up Top News but can quickly and easily jump between it and your Most Recent or other filtered information.

By selecting a filter other than most recent, you can see the latest updates for just that specific type of information. The filters you have available to you change depending on what games and apps you subscribe to on Facebook.

WHAT IF I WANT TO SEE MORE OF MY NEWS FEED? A limited amount of page real estate is available in your browser, so if you want to see more of your News Feed, scroll down to the bottom, and click Older Posts to load up more posts.

To control what types of information, what friends, and what specific posts appear in your News Feed, follow these steps:

1. Hover your cursor over the center News Feed column. You should then see an X appear along the top of each specific News Feed.

2. Click the X and a drop-down appears with several options. These actions include hiding a post, hiding all posts from that friend, hiding all posts related to a specific game or app, unliking a page (assuming you previously chose to Like it, which is described later in this chapter), and marking as spam. The available actions change depending on the friend and type of post that was made.

3. Click the action you want to take, and it will be performed.

WHY ARE STORIES APPEARING FROM PEOPLE WHO ARE NOT MY FRIENDS? You may see some stories appearing in your News Feed from other people who are not your friends if your friends have liked or interacted with the post and if that person's privacy settings are set to everyone or friends of friends.

One of the quickest ways to share something is by using one of the five available Share links centered at the top of your News Feed (the Publisher area). You can share your status, pose a question, and share a photo, link, or video from this quick access area. You also have the ability to customize who sees the information you are sharing by clicking the Lock icon next to the word Share. Following are available options:

+ **Status:** Simply enter your status in the Text field, and click the Share button.

+ **Question**: This new Share option enables you to pose a question to your friends and also add a poll to your question. This is a fun way to generate some conversations.

+ **Photo:** As shown in Figure 3-5 you can click to upload a photo from your computer, take a photo with your webcam, or create an album with many photos. Chapter 6 (How Do I Share Photos and Videos?) discusses photo and video sharing in detail.

+ **Link:** You can share links with people using this option, covered in detail next.

+ **Video:** Click to record a video with your webcam or upload a video from your drive.

Facebook has a slick way to share links with people that makes it more useful than simply posting a link to your News Feed. Follow these steps to share a link:

1. Click the Link option in the Share area.

2. Enter a URL in the text box.

3. Click the Attach button. A title, the URL, a thumbnail image, and some text from the URL page should now appear.

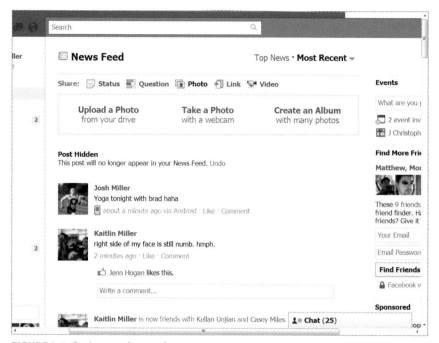

FIGURE 3-5 Options to share a photo

4. Use the arrow buttons to choose a thumbnail to associate with the shared link, or choose to have no thumbnail attached.

5. Enter some text to share with your friends along with the link, such as "I loved this story, so check it out."

6. Click the Lock icon in the bottom right to select who will receive your share link. You can also leave it at the default.

7. Click the Share button to share the link with your friends.

- -

LIMITING YOUR NEWS FEED You might also want to limit posts in your News Feed; click the Edit Options hyperlink in the bottom right to control who you see feeds from on a global basis.

- -

Down the Right Side

The right column is a fairly consistent column divided into five sections, as shown in Figure 3-6. If you have no pending events, requests, or pokes, these sections will not appear in your right side column.

- **Events:** Upcoming events appear with a hyperlink option to see all.
- **Sponsored:** Facebook Ads appear here; these cannot be removed.
- **Requests:** Pending requests appear here with the number pending and an option to see all.
- **Pokes:** Received pokes appear in this section with a quick link option to poke back.
- **Get Connected:** Several suggested methods to discover new connections are listed in this bottom section.

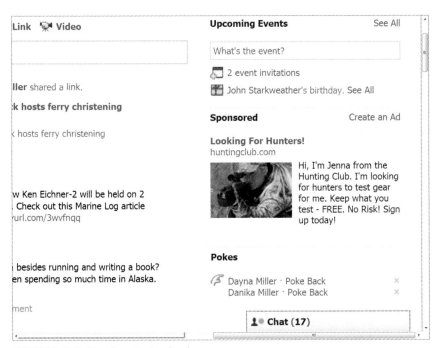

FIGURE 3-6 Right column in Facebook

ISN'T IT RUDE TO POKE SOMEONE? Physical pokes can be rude, but in Facebook a *poke* is simply a quick way to say hello; when you poke people, they receive an alert on their home page. You may want to poke someone you see sleeping in a meeting, use it to initiate a conversation, or just do it to bug your friend.

Although seeing ads on Facebook in the Sponsored section may get annoying, remember that Facebook is free and stores an incredible amount of data with servers and people that work hard to provide you with these services. You can click the X to remove an ad you do not like, but you can't get rid of these completely. Alternately, you can even create your own ad, which Chapter 14 (How Can I Use Facebook to Build and Promote My Business?) covers. If you do click to remove an ad, you see a quick dropdown survey about why you removed it that includes the following:

+ Uninteresting
+ Misleading
+ Offensive
+ Repetitive
+ Other

Answering this survey will help Facebook cater their ads more to your liking.

Chat Area

Facebook is a powerful social network platform that also supports the ability to instant message with your friends. Chapter 5 (How Do I Communicate With Friends?) offers details on using chat, but you can find the Chat area in the bottom-right corner of your web browser, as shown in Figure 3-7. By default, it appears simply as a small box with your status, offline or online, appearing.

When you click the word chat, your status changes to online if you were offline, and a long box showing your online friends and their status—available or idle—appears. You can then hold chat sessions with them or control your online and offline status. Chat is active two way communications where both parties must be online to interact.

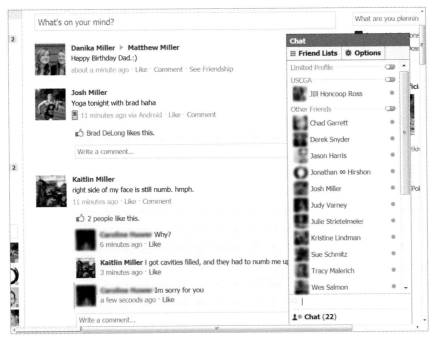

FIGURE 3-7 Chat area in bottom-right corner

Like Button

Throughout the Facebook site you see the word Like next to posts, photos, videos, and more. Like is a way to give positive feedback to something you enjoy. You can also Like things you see on your Friends page, and then that action will be pulled into your News Feed and shared with your friends.

You cannot "dislike" something, but you can choose to Unlike something after you Like it; this simply means you want to stop liking it and not that you dislike it.

Notifications

The best place to see new notifications is in the top blue bar where the Globe icon sits to the left of the search box. When new notifications pop up, a red number appears letting you know how many are waiting for you to read. This same type of notification appears for messages you receive as well (see Figure 3-8).

FIGURE 3-8 Received a new notification

As described in this chapter, other areas are available in your left and right columns where notifications related to specific types of information appear, such as events, messages, and pokes. You may also have notifications set up to be sent to you via email or text message, and these settings are available on your Account Settings page under the Notifications tab.

Navigating Your Profile Page

Your Profile page, shown in Figure 3-9, is set up a bit differently than the main Facebook home page. You still see the universal top blue bar and have the same controls there, however; you can find a slightly different left column that has quick access to your Wall (collection of your status updates, shared items, and profile updates), info, photos, notes, friends, and groups. This column is about you and not your friends because you are on your Profile page.

The center column contains your profile summary, recently tagged photos, and a Share area just like on your home page News Feed; the rest of the column is filled with all your latest Facebook activity.

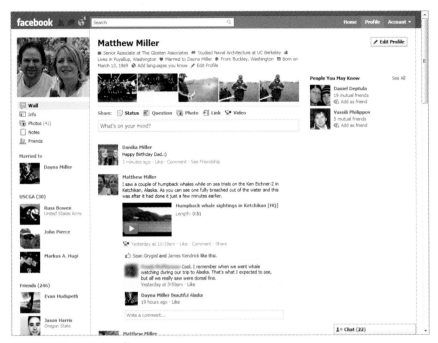

FIGURE 3-9 Typical Profile page

The Profile page is a handy way to show what you have been doing and to go back to see what your friends have been commenting on as related to your updates only.

Examining the 2011 User Interface

For several years Facebook has had a multiple column layout, but in December of 2010 it changed the user interface, including what appears in those columns and how some of the interaction controls work. Some of the more recent and radical changes include the following:

- **Top menu blue bar:** One of the biggest changes to the top menu is that the Notifications icon moved from the lower-right corner of the page to the top menu, as described at the beginning of this chapter. I find this to be a thousand times more useful as my eye tends to look up and to the left rather than down in the bottom right where I place less value.

✛ **Facebook Photos:** When you now click to view a photo, the photo appears as a large pop-up over the top of your browser, so you can see the full photo, associated comments, and other ways to interact with the photo for tagging, liking, and more. I like the way you can now scroll through photos in this additional layer without losing your place on the Facebook page.

✛ **Updated Profile:** The profile update that started rolling out in late 2010 is one of the more radical updates in a while on Facebook. You now see a quick summary of information about you and a filmstrip of photos you have recently been tagged in. You can also manage featured friends, including family members. The tabs that were at the top of your profile are now along the left side, which actually makes it a bit more of a consistent experience with the standard Facebook home page. Facebook also added new fields for your interests, a new graphic display for your top interests, and more ways to list how you spend your time.

✛ **Wall not as prominent:** The Wall used to be a rather prominent feature of Facebook but has now been rolled into and integrated more into your profile without having such a defined separate location.

This is not the first time Facebook has improved their UI to facilitate navigation and discovery of functions, and it may not be the last. To stay abreast of the changes and new features that Facebook has recently added or will add in the future, visit the Facebook blog at `http://blog.facebook.com/`.

Related Questions

✛ How many friends can I chat with at the same time? **PAGES 61 AND 174**

✛ Where can I get applications like the ones in your left column? **PAGE 181**

✛ How can I set up an event like you show in the right column? **PAGE 95**

CHAPTER FOUR

HOW DO I FIND AND ADD FRIENDS?

Y ou now have a Facebook account, set-up your own profile, and know how to get around the site, so it is time to add some friends and expand your social network. You likely want to start by adding your close family and friends, some of whom may have encouraged you to join Facebook in the first place, to get a better feel for Facebook and see what your limits are for privacy, sharing information, and using the social network to connect with others. A few different ways exist to find people, suggest friends to others, join a network of friends, and block people who you do not want to ever be friends with.

Use Facebook Search

One of the most powerful and quickest ways to find people on Facebook is to simply search for them. You must have a Facebook account and be signed in to use the Search tool, so after logging in, follow these steps to initiate a search for a high school or college classmate, old girlfriend or boyfriend, a family member, or anyone else you prefer.

1. Locate the search box in the top center of your Facebook page and place your cursor in the box.

2. Start typing a person's name. You see that Facebook starts auto-filling out names as you enter text, (see Figure 4-1). Facebook shows the top eight results, including people you already are friends with, if applicable. This enables you to use the search box as a way to quickly jump to a friend's profile in addition to searching for people you are not friends with.

3. If the person's name appears in the quick list, simply click on it to go to her page where you can see her profile.

4. You can then send a friend request, as discussed in the next section.

- -

FRIEND NOT IN THE TOP EIGHT LISTED? If the person you are searching for is not in the top eight shown in the list, look down at the bottom to see a link for viewing more results. Simply click this to see the full Search Results page, as shown in Figure 4-2.

- -

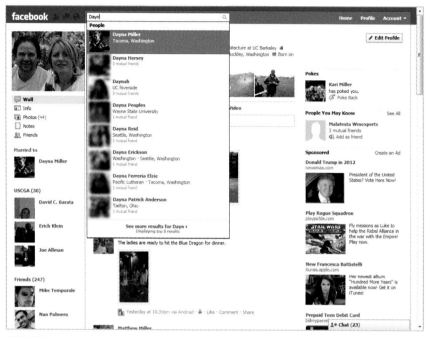

FIGURE 4-1 Using the search function

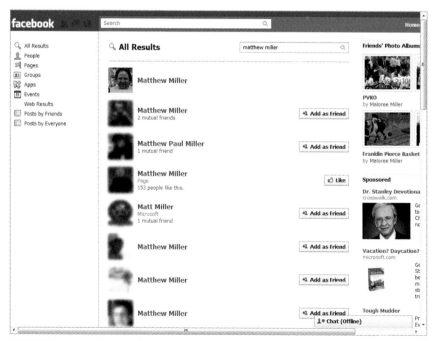

FIGURE 4-2 Friend Search Results page

Searching in the search box not only searches for people, but can also provide you quick access to groups, applications, and pages. These types of results are discussed more in Chapters 11, 12, and 13.

LOOK THROUGH YOUR FRIENDS' LISTS You can also find friends by simply browsing through your existing friends' list of friends. If you find someone there you want to befriend, simply perform the following steps to send a friend request.

SEND A FRIEND REQUEST

After you conduct a search and find the person you want to connect with, simply click the button to Add as Friend. You can do this from the Search Results list or from the potential friend's Facebook page. After clicking to Add as Friend, follow these steps:

1. In the pop-up box, as shown in Figure 4-3, you have the option to add the person to one of your lists. This is completely optional, but can help you keep your friends organized.

2. You can also check the box to subscribe to this person's feeds via SMS. Again, this is completely optional.

3. You also have the option to add a personal message to a request rather than the default request. To do this, simply click this option and enter some text.

4. The one mandatory step to complete this action is to click the Send Request button. After clicking this button, a pop-up appears stating that your request was sent.

After you send out requests, acceptances will appear in your Notifications area.

WHAT IF I CHANGE MY MIND? If you decide that sending a request to someone wasn't the best idea, you can visit her profile and click the button to Cancel Friend Request.

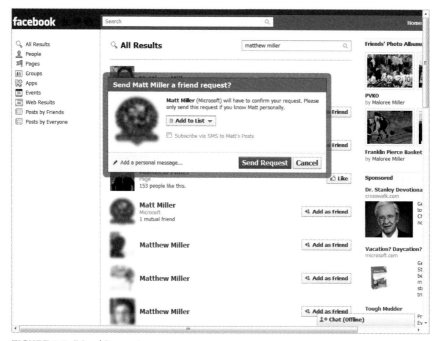

FIGURE 4-3 Friend Request pop-up

INVITE FRIENDS VIA THIRD-PARTY CONTACT LISTS

You can also use the power of your various contact lists to invite people to Facebook to be your friend. Follow these steps to use your contact lists:

1. Click Friends in the left column of your Facebook page.

2. Click the Edit Friends button in the top right.

3. Click Invite Friends in the left column.

4. Enter email addresses for friends you want to invite or use the automatic Invite tool for Windows Live Hotmail, AOL Mail, or Yahoo! Mail on the right side, as shown in Figure 4-4.

5. After entering email addresses, write a message, and then click the Invite button to send out the invites.

FIGURE 4-4 Invite Your Friends entry page

You also see the Find Friends option in the left column after getting to the Friends management page found after following Steps 1 and 2 above. If you click this Find Friends link you see a list of different services through which you can sign in and look for more friends. These services include Windows Live Messenger, Yahoo!, Skype, and more.

Respond to Friend Requests

Other people are also likely looking for friends, and as a result, you will surely receive friend requests at some point. You can choose to confirm that friend request, delete the request, or defer the request until a later time. It is impossible to become friends with someone on Facebook without both users confirming the connection through initiating or receiving friend requests. Someone else cannot make the connection for you, so you should feel safe managing your own Friend list.

CONFIRM A FRIEND REQUEST

The easiest (and most common) action to take regarding friend requests is to confirm (accept) them. If you choose to accept the person as a friend, the person will be added to your Friend list, and you can visit it to add them to a group if you like. You will now have access to write on their wall, comment on their pictures, and receive notification of their status updates, among other things.

DEFER OR DELETE A FRIEND REQUEST

If you don't want to confirm a friend request you can choose to defer it by selecting Not Now. If you defer it, the request goes into your requests list. You can revisit it later by following these steps:

1. Click the people icon in the top left of your upper blue bar.

2. Click on See All Friend Requests. Another page opens up with a list of requests you have not taken action on. If you do not see any here you may have to click See Hidden Requests.

3. You will now see options to Confirm or Delete Request for each specific person that sent you a request. You also have the option to Delete All of these requests with a single click.

4. If you select Delete Request you will see a question under the person's name asking, "Don't know John Smith?" If you click on this link then they will be blocked from sending you future requests; if you don't click the link they can send you another request.

- -

WILL THE PERSON KNOW I DELETED THEIR REQUEST? If you feel bad for deleting a request, don't worry. The people sending them won't receive a notification saying you deleted the request; when they eventually look for your profile again they will just see a grey box indicating Friend Request Sent.

- -

If you are bothered with lots of friend requests and want to take more global actions, you can change the setting for receipt of friend requests in your privacy settings. See Chapter 8 (How Do I Optimize My Privacy Settings?) for more details on these settings.

Suggest Friends to Others

You may wonder how some people find you on Facebook; one way this can happen is through a suggestion from another friend. If you have existing Facebook friends and know some others might benefit and appreciate having one of them as a friend, you can choose to suggest the person to others.

To suggest friends to others, follow these steps:

1. Visit the Profile page of one of your friends.

2. Look in the bottom left; click the Suggest Friends button. A pop-up box appears with all your Facebook friends on it, as shown in Figure 4-5. Facebook will even recommend friends for you to suggest based on common friends, your address book, schools, employers, and other demographic data Facebook captures from your profile.

3. You can either click your friends' profile pictures or enter a name and filter to them in the text box. Select the friends who you want to suggest to the friend whose profile you are viewing. A check mark appears in the bottom-left corner on the profile picture of the friends you choose to suggest.

FIGURE 4-5 Suggest Friends pop-up selector

4. Click Send Suggestions to recommend this friend to others.

The ability to suggest friends to others is a handy and quick way to connect with school classmates and other groups of people who may know each other.

Join a Network

You can also expand and discover people through the school you attend or place you work. Network connections can be made only through valid email addresses, and you can have only up to five networks on your account. To join a network, follow these steps:

1. Click My Account.
2. Click the Network tab.
3. Enter a workplace or school in the box.
4. Click Join Network.

You must have a valid education institution email address to join a school network. If you try to join through your place of business, it must have set up a network and distributed email addresses, too.

People within your network can see your profile by default, so if you want to change this, you need to edit your privacy settings, as covered in Chapter 8 (How Do I Optimize My Privacy Settings?).

Block People

Not everything is rosy in this world, and you might find that you need to block some people from your Facebook life. Blocking people prevents them from viewing your profile, and any existing friend connections will be broken. You will not appear in their search results or Friend lists either, so you should be virtually invisible to them. After blocking someone, they too become invisible to you because blocking is a two-way street, much like becoming friends with people.

CAN I UNFRIEND PEOPLE? If you don't want to be friends with someone anymore, but you don't want to go as far as to block them, you can remove people from your Friend list by navigating to their profile and clicking the Unfriend button on the left side of their page. They will know this happened because you will also be removed from their Friend list, so make sure this is something you want to do before clicking too quickly. They won't receive a notification but may see the changes if they browse their Friend list and notice you aren't on it.

There are a few instances in which you may come into contact with someone you have previously blocked. These include the following:

- ✛ **Via third party applications**: For example, you may be playing a game with multiple players hosted by a mutual friend and thus a person you blocked may be in that same game as you.

- ✛ **Through comments**: You may also see a blocked person's comments, and vice-versa, if you have mutual friends.

Therefore, blocking does indeed prevent direct interaction, but it is not completely universal in nature.

WILL SOMEONE KNOW IF I BLOCK THEM? Similar to unfriending, people will not know that you have blocked them through a notification, but you will not appear in their searches, so they may figure it out.

Now that you know the limitations and what blocking does, see the following to learn the different ways to block a Facebook user.

- ✛ Go to the Block Lists from Your Privacy Settings page, and enter the name or email address of the person you want to block. Then click Block.

- ✛ Go to his Profile page; look down toward the bottom for the Report/ Block This Person link. Click the link, check the box to Block This Person, and click Continue, as shown in Figure 4-6.

- ✛ If you received a Message from this person directly, visit a message and look on the right side of the message header. Click the Report link, check the box to Block This Person, and then click Submit.

FIGURE 4-6 Options available to block people

CAN I UNBLOCK SOMEONE? If you change your mind later, you can visit your privacy settings and edit your block lists. You can find a link to the block lists and at the bottom of your Privacy Settings page.

Related Questions

➕ How can I manage the details of my privacy settings? **PAGE 109**

➕ Where do notifications of friend requests appear? **PAGE 37**

➕ How can I turn a new friend into a Featured Friend? **PAGE 16**

CHAPTER FIVE

HOW DO I COMMUNICATE WITH FRIENDS?

In this chapter:

+ The Wall
+ Send Messages
+ Chat
+ Poke Friends
+ Groups
+ Tag Friends

O ne of the primary reasons for having a Facebook account is to communicate with your family and friends. In this chapter you look at various ways
to stay in touch through the Wall, comments, private messages, live chat,
pokes, groups, and tagging. Communication can be private, public, and even
semi-public, depending on the form of communication that you use through
Facebook.

The Wall

As described in Chapter 3 (How Do I Navigate Facebook?), there is a place in the
center column where you can quickly enter some text, upload/take a photo,
attach a link, or upload/take a video, and share it with your Facebook friends.
When you share from this area, you are posting this information to your Wall.
This is made even clearer if you go to your Profile page where you can see the
top hyperlink in the left column labeled Wall, as shown in Figure 5-1. The Wall
icon is a set of double quotation marks with a green background, so in your
recent activity you can tell which actions took place on your Wall.

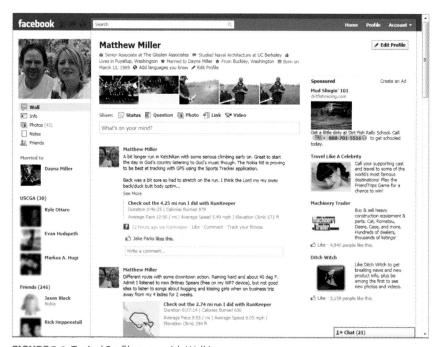

FIGURE 5-1 Typical Profile page with Wall icons

WHAT ARE MEMORABLE STATUS UPDATES? While visiting a friend's Facebook page you may occasionally see a section in the right column showing past status updates or photos from that person. This is a fun way to call attention to long-forgotten wall posts. As of April 2011 there is no known way to designate memorable status updates or control when they appear.

By default, when you post on your Wall, your post is shared out to everyone. You should visit your privacy settings to control who can see your Wall posts and who can comment on your Wall posts. You can also use the Groups feature (see Chapter 11 [What Are Groups and How Can I Use Them?]) to post comments to a group of people.

WHAT IS THE DIFFERENCE BETWEEN A STATUS UPDATE AND A NEWS FEED? Status updates are the Wall posts that you make on your own Wall that appear in a chronological order with no importance assigned. News Feed is a list of activity, including status updates, from people and Pages that you follow on Facebook created with an algorithm that brings the most interesting content to the top of the list. The algorithm is based on how many friends are commenting on the content, who posted it, and what type it is.

You can also write or share something with a friend by posting on her Wall. Friends of friends can see Wall posts you make, so if you want to post something private, use the Messages function discussed in the next section of this chapter. To post on a friend's Wall, follow these steps:

1. Open the Profile page of one of your friends.
2. Look in the center of your display, and under your friend's profile summary and profile pictures, see the Share area.
3. Enter text in the box containing the grayed out words Write Something, as shown in Figure 5-2; then click Share to post on your friend's Wall.

Similar to when you post on your own Wall, you can upload photos, links, and videos to your friend's Wall as well.

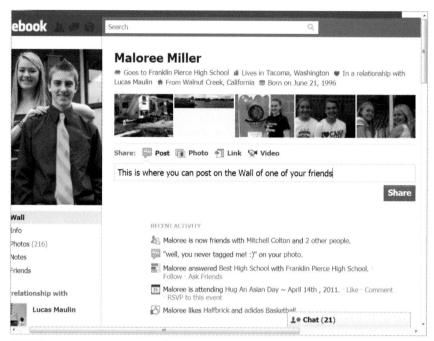

FIGURE 5-2 Entering a post on a friend's Wall

WHY CAN'T I WRITE ON SOME OF MY FRIENDS' WALLS? Your friends can manage their own privacy settings, and in some cases people block others from posting on their Wall.

You can also comment on your friend's status update simply by entering a comment in the text entry field where the words "Write a comment" appear. After you post a comment you have the ability to delete it by tapping on the X to the right of your comment.

HOW CAN I ENTER MORE THAN ONE PARAGRAPH IN MY COMMENT?
If you enter text in comment block on your friend's Wall and press enter, your comment uploads. If you want to enter multiple paragraphs, you need to press Shift+Enter to stay within the text field and enter more text.

Send Messages

Facebook is a complete platform that includes the capability to send and receive messages privately, similar to an email system or direct message on Twitter. Facebook started rolling out a newer version of Messages in early 2011 that includes access to all your private conversations in one place. This includes chats, texts, messages, and email (if you choose to create a free @facebook.com address). This updated version is rolling out on an incremental basis; if you want to speed up this process, you can upgrade at www.facebook .com/pages/browser.php#!/about/messages/.

The previous version of Messages focused on just messages that you send back and forth through Facebook rather than offering the integrated experience, but the functionality for messages is the same in both versions.

To view all your messages and either send a new message or respond to current messages, click the word Messages in your left column of your Home Page. Your messages then appear in the center column of your Facebook page, as shown in Figure 5-3.

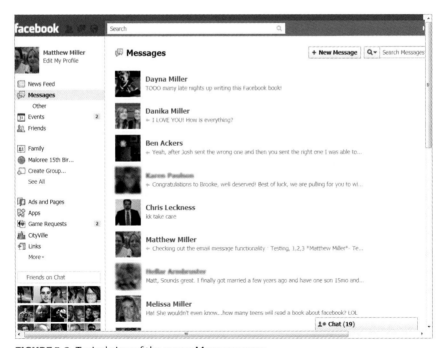

FIGURE 5-3 Typical view of the newer Messages page

To send a new message, follow these steps:

1. Click the New Message button in the upper-right corner.

2. Start typing a name to have Facebook auto-filter your Friends list until the person you want to share with appears. You can enter multiple friends in your message, too. There is a limit of 20 recipients in a Facebook message.

3. Enter the text of your message in the message text box.

4. Click the Paper Clip or Camera icon in the bottom left to attach a link, photo, or video. This is optional.

5. Click the Phone icon in the bottom right to send this message as a text message to your friend as well. This is also optional.

There are shortcuts to do this, however; if you just want to send a message, the easiest ways is to follow these simple steps:

1. Find a friend's post in your News Feed or Status Update in the center of your page.

2. Hover your mouse over her name.

3. Click the left-bottom hyperlink to Send Message. A To: line appears with your friend's name in it above a Message entry box (see Figure 5-4).

4. Enter a message, and then click Send message to send it to your friend.

WHAT'S UP WITH THIS @FACEBOOK.COM EMAIL OPTION? You can choose to enable a free @facebook.com email address that uses your profile username so that you will have username@facebook.com. People can then email you at this address and have the email appear in your Messages section. Outgoing emails you send look like Facebook messages, including your name, profile picture, and your message.

WHAT IS THE SUBHEADING "OTHER" USED FOR? With the newer version of Messages, you see an Other subheading under Messages in the left hand column of your Facebook page. Clicking this link lists messages you receive through events, groups, and other applications that are not direct communications between friends, such as bulk items not easily identifiable as individuals.

FIGURE 5-4 Entering a new message

If you have been carrying on a conversation with someone via messages, an easy way to continue this discussion is to simply click the person's name on the Messages page and enter a message in the text box that your cursor automatically moves to at the bottom of the page. The addressee is the person you clicked, so you can save two steps using this method; plus, it turns into a threaded conversation similar to a chat session.

Chat

Facebook Chat is an instant message (IM) client that requires both parties to be connected to Facebook at the same time. My favorite part about Facebook Chat is that practically all of my family and friends are already on it. This way, I don't have to figure out what IM service my different friends use; instead I only have to go to one place to chat with them all!

CAN I USE FACEBOOK CHAT ON MY SMARTPHONE? As discussed in Chapter 9 (How Can I Use Facebook Effectively on My Mobile Phone?), even some mobile clients enable you to use Chat on the go.

As discussed in Chapter 3 (How Do I Navigate Facebook?), Facebook Chat is easily accessed through the following steps:

1. Look to the bottom right of your Facebook page and click the word Chat (Offline).

2. Clicking this automatically logs you in and changes your status to Online (see Figure 5-5). Your Facebook friends can then see your status change to a green circle and initiate a chat session with you.

FIGURE 5-5 Chat status window

CHAT OPTIONS

The first thing I do after signing in to Chat is to go to the upper right of the chat window and click Options. You can also choose from the following options:

+ Reorder lists (clicking lets you drag to reorder groups).

+ Pop out Chat (pops out a window for Chat sessions).

+ Play sound for new messages.

+ Keep online friends window open.

+ Show only names in online friends (rather than including their profile picture, too).

Here you also can switch to offline mode and log out of Chat.

INITIATING AND HOLDING A CHAT SESSION

Your friends appear with either a green circle icon or a partial moon icon to the right of their name. If your friends are not in the list, they are offline and unavailable for any Chat sessions. Those with a green circle are online and available to chat. Those with the partial moon are currently idle. A person's status changes to idle if he has not taken any action on Facebook within the last 10 minutes. Thus, you may carry out a Chat session with an idle friend if he responds to a message you send.

- -

CAN I CHAT WITH MORE THAN ONE PERSON IN THE SAME CONVERSATION? Yes; you can use Group chats in Facebook. Go to a Group page, click Chat with Group in the right column under the list of Group members, and then hold a live Chat session. Learn more about Group Chat in Chapter 11 (What are Groups and How Can I Use Them?).

- -

To start a Chat session, simply click on a person in your Chat list, enter some text in the text box, and then press Enter to send your message. You notice that you can carry on multiple Chat sessions and that each one appears with your friend's name along the bottom of your display.

You can also easily create Friend lists within Chat, so you can have easy filters for your friends. You can use Friend lists in chat to help you manage your Chat sessions in a few different ways:

+ Click on Friend Lists and toggle on or off existing lists to filter out your Chat list.

+ Click on Friend Lists and create a new list right from within the Chat window.

+ Tap the green horizontal toggle switch at the top of a Friend List to appear offline just to those people on that particular list.

You can also use emoticons in your conversation to add some emotions to your text. Emoticons are facial expressions or characters that are created using different forms of punctuation or letters. For example, a smiley face is created with a colon and a parenthesis, like so :). When you type these different emoticon combinations in a Facebook Chat Window, however, they turn into animated pictures, such as yellow faces, penguins, or even sharks! Go to http://facebookemoticons.com/emoticons/ to learn all the different pictures you can make and the keyboard combinations that create them.

- -

CAN I SEND A PICTURE OVER CHAT? Pictures, video, and other attachments cannot be used in Chat and should be used through the Messaging functionality.

- -

As previously mentioned, the 2011 Messages UI enables you to have Chat sessions integrated into your Messages view for a better conversation experience.

Poke Friends

Do you get annoyed with Facebook friends who won't get online to chat or who don't seem to be interacting with you as much as you would like? Facebook designed the Poke feature to serve as a nudge so you can get your friend's attention and hopefully get them to respond. When you poke someone, they receive a Poke Alert in their right column with a quick option to poke you back.

To poke a friend, follow these steps:

1. Go to a friend's Facebook page.

2. Look at the upper-right portion of her page, and click the Poke button. A confirmation pop-up box appears informing you of what is going to happen (see Figure 5-6).

3. Click the Poke button in the pop-up box to send the poke to your friend.

FIGURE 5-6 Creating a Poke

Tag Friends

Your Facebook friends often post photos on their pages and may even share them with you. If you browse photos and notice some of your Facebook friends in the photo, you can easily tag the people in that photo as a way to communicate to them that they are in a photo on Facebook.

To tag a photo with someone, follow these steps:

1. Find a photo with one of your Facebook friends in it.

2. Click the Tag This Photo link in the lower-right column under the photo.

3. Click a person's face in the photo.

4. Type her name in the box as shown in Figure 5-7, and Facebook auto-completes your entry with friends of yours who match that name. Press enter when you find the right person. If the name of your friend doesn't appear, they may not be on Facebook, or you may not be friends with them. If you press Enter, the name you entered still appears under the picture, just without a hyperlink.

5. Click Done Tagging when you finish tagging your friend.

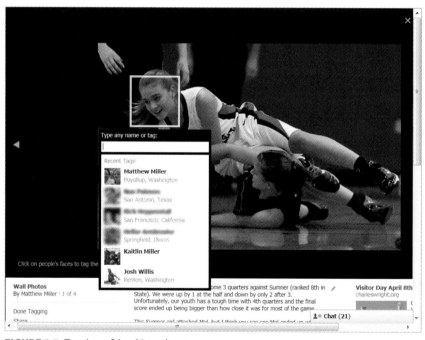

FIGURE 5-7 Tagging a friend in a photo

Facebook then sends a notice to both the person who you tagged in the photo, and the person who owns and originally posted the photo, including a link to that photo. This tag can also appear in the Recent Activity section of the tagged person's profile. The person then has the option to view the photo and remove the tag if it is incorrect or if she does not want to be tagged in that photo.

Related Questions

+ How can I communicate with my friends from my smartphone? **PAGE 128**

+ How can I communicate with a secret Group? **PAGE 170**

+ How do I share a photo so that I can tag my friends in it? **PAGES 68 AND 79**

CHAPTER SIX

HOW DO I SHARE PHOTOS AND VIDEOS?

Chapter 1 (Why Choose Facebook and How Do I Get Started?) mentions that you can use Facebook to interact and share your life with your family and friends, and a great way to do that is with photos and videos. Several online photo services are available, but Facebook brings a major social network element to the party and is quickly becoming "the place" to share your photos. You can organize photos of your family and friends in albums, comment on photos, change your profile picture, and even perform some basic photo editing in Facebook. You can also share videos directly on Facebook, through an external host such as YouTube, and even send video messages to people. Photos and videos are easy to share within Facebook and lots of fun to view.

Sharing Photos

According to a report by Pixable (`http://tinyurl.com/469xatu`) 60 billion (yes, billion) photos were uploaded to Facebook by the end of 2010, with 6 billion photos uploaded each month. This means that by mid-2011 there should be 100 billion photos uploaded to Facebook. For comparison, Pixable reports that PhotoBucket had 8 billion uploads, Picasa 7 billion, and Flickr 5 billion by the end of 2010. Photos is an application in Facebook and appears along with videos in your Profile area, as shown in Figure 6-1.

UPLOAD A PHOTO FROM YOUR DRIVE

The following explains how easy it is to upload a photo from your computer to Facebook. (To see how to do it from your phone, check out Chapter 9, [How Can I Use Facebook Effectively on My Mobile Phone?])

1. On your main Facebook home page or Profile page, click the Photo icon/link in the Share area in the center of the display. Three photo options appear after clicking Photo, as shown in Figure 6-2. Choose Upload a Photo from your drive.

2. Click the Choose File or Browse button. A file explorer interface appears. Navigate to the photo you want to upload and double click it or click Open to select it.

3. Enter something about the photo into the text box with the words, "Say something about this photo...."

4. Click Share to post the photo.

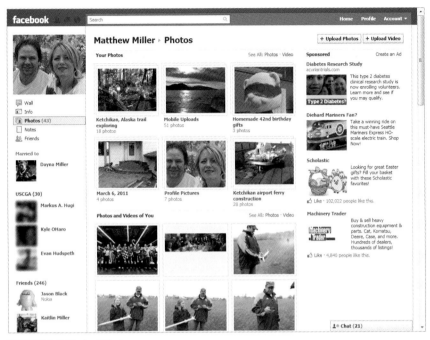

FIGURE 6-1 Typical Photos page

FIGURE 6-2 Photo sharing options

PHOTO UPLOAD ISSUES? CHECK OUT THESE TIPS Facebook recommends that you upload photos up to 720 x 720 pixels with a total size that does not exceed 15MB. However, you can upload larger images if you have the patience for them to upload. Facebook also recommends using .jpg, .bmp, .png, .gif, and .tiff image formats because they have limits on supported file types.

UPLOAD VIA EMAIL AS AN OPTION During the upload process, you can click a hyperlink to upload via email instead of choosing a file. If you click this Facebook provides you with a unique email address to where you can simply send photos to get posted. Keep this email a secret or others can upload photos to your account.

The photo now appears on your Wall with the ability for people to Like, Comment, or Share it, as shown in Figure 6-3. Some editing functions are also available that are discussed in the "Edit and Tag Photos" section.

FIGURE 6-3 Uploaded photo in Facebook Photo Viewer

TAKE A PHOTO WITH A WEBCAM

You likely also notice the option to Take a Photo with a webcam after you click the Photo option in your Share area. The first thing you need on your computer is either an integrated webcam or external webcam to consider using this option. Assuming that you do have a connected webcam, see the following on how to upload a photo using this method.

1. On your main Facebook home page or Profile page, click the Photo icon/link in the Share area in the center of the display and choose Take a Photo with a webcam.

2. Align the subject of the picture with your webcam, and click the Camera icon to start the timer to capture the photo. A 3-second countdown begins and then a photo is taken.

3. Enter something about the photo into the text box with the words, "Say something about this photo...."

4. Click Share to post the photo.

FLASH PLAYER ALERT The first time you choose to upload via a webcam photo, you might see an Adobe Flash Player privacy pop-up. If you want to allow Facebook to access your camera and microphone, click to Allow this access to use your webcam.

You can also have a lot of fun with the effects on your webcam in Facebook. In the upper-left corner of the webcam capture area, notice a drop-down list for different filters. You have the following options:

+ No filter
+ Blur
+ Sharpen
+ Contrast
+ Edges
+ Grayscale
+ Solarize

✦ Fog

✦ Twirl

✦ Fisheye

✦ Pinch

As you select each one, you see the effect live in the webcam viewfinder area. Select different ones and move around in the viewfinder to create some crazy photos to share with family and friends.

CREATE AN ALBUM WITH MANY PHOTOS

The two methods detailed earlier relate to sharing a single photo on your Wall. If you have a collection of photos that you want to share, not via the webcam, you can create an album and select photos to go into it. There is a 200-photo limit per album, so if you try to upload more than 200, you see an error message. Take these steps to create an album, and populate it with photos.

1. On your main Facebook home page or Profile page, click the Photo icon/link in the Share area in the center of the display, and choose Create an Album with many photos.

2. Click Select Photos from the pop-up screen. A file explorer interface appears. Navigate to the photos you want to upload, and click on them. You can use the traditional Shift +Ctrl (Command for Mac) functions for selecting several adjacent or several specific files in this selection interface.

3. Click Open to select the photos and a window showing the upload status appears. Here you can enter the name of the album, location, and quality (standard or high resolution) and who to share the album with. Make your selections and enter the information you want.

4. Click Create Album. You also have the option at this time to click Cancel Upload if you change your mind about the album and do not want to post it.

5. Another page, similar to the one shown in Figure 6-4, appears with options to edit your album. A highlighted note states that the photos

have not yet been published with buttons to Publish Now or Skip this editing step. Editing options include:

+ Add photo descriptions

+ Tag friends

+ Select a photo for the album cover

+ Delete selected photos

+ Move the photo(s) to a different album

Make your edits; then click Publish Now to share your updated album.

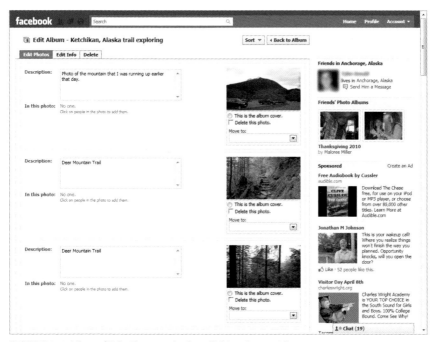

FIGURE 6-4 View of Edit Photos tab after clicking Create Album

SIMPLE UPLOADER In the pop-up that appears after choosing Create an Album, you see the option to use the Simple Uploader if you have trouble using the default selector. Click this link and follow the steps on the new Album creation page that appears instead of a pop-up if you have upload issues.

Remember that whenever you get ready to click the Share button for any type of Wall post, you have the option to the left of the button to change the privacy settings for that particular Wall post, as shown in Figure 6-5. Therefore, you can manage who sees a particular photo album separately from what people see as status updates on your Wall.

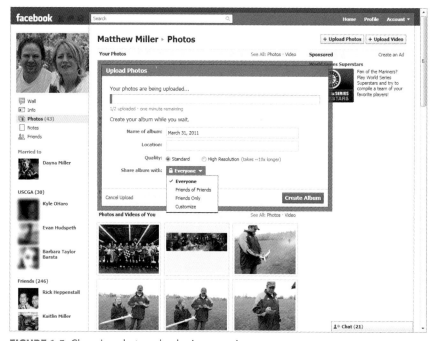

FIGURE 6-5 Changing photo upload privacy settings

You may also want to add photos to an existing album, and as long as you don't have more than 200 photos in the album, you can do so. To add more photos, follow these steps:

1. Click the Photos link on your Facebook Profile page.

2. Select one of your existing albums.

3. Click the Add More Photos button.

4. From the pop-up screen, click the Select Photos button.

5. Follow Steps 3-6 from the preceding description of how to create an album with many photos.

Some albums are created automatically. For these selected albums you do not see the ability to add more photos. These albums are created depending on how the photos were uploaded. These include:

+ **Wall Photos**: Created automatically when you follow the process for uploading a single photo via your computer or one captured via webcam.

+ **Mobile Uploads**: Created when you upload from your mobile phone, as discussed further in Chapter 9, (How Can I Use Facebook Effectively on My Mobile Phone?) or via the special email address mentioned earlier in the Upload Photos section.

+ **Profile Pictures**: Created with each new profile photo you upload or assign.

There is a limit of 100 photos in the Mobile Uploads album, but as soon as you hit that, Facebook creates another Mobile Uploads album and adds the next 100 to that.

SEND A PHOTO IN A MESSAGE

The photos you upload and share individually or in an album are generally designed to be shared with a large number of your Facebook friends. You may find times when you want to share a photo directly with a specific person in a private conversation, and you can do this through Messages.

To include a photo in a private message to a specific person(s), follow these steps:

1. Compose a new message to a friend; see Chapter 5 (How Do I Communicate with Friends?) for detailed steps on how to create messages.

2. In the New Message pop-up window, click the paperclip icon to attach a photo stored on your computer, or click the Camera icon to take a webcam photo, as shown in Figure 6-6. (In the older messages UI, click the photo icon to the right of Attach in the bottom left; there is no webcam option in this UI).

3. After including a photo, click Send to send the message to your friend.

FIGURE 6-6 Taking a webcam photo to include in a message

CAN I FILTER WEBCAM PHOTOS? Photos captured with your webcam for Messages do not have the capability to apply filters.

SHARE A PHOTO OR ALBUM

The ability to see all your posted photos depends on the privacy settings you set up for your Facebook account. If you have a specific photo or album that you want to make sure selected friends can see, you can choose to share a photo or album with these friends. You may also share friends' photos or albums. To share a photo, follow these steps:

   1. Find a photo you want to share and click it. You see the photo open up over the top of your Facebook page.

2. In the bottom left of the photo viewer, click Share.

3. You can then enter in some text with your thoughts on the photo, and click Share or choose to send the photo as a Message directly to specific people.

This process is great for sharing a photo you found on someone else's page, but you can also use it to share a photo that you created just to give a bit of emphasis to it and to make it fresh on your Wall again.

SHARING DOESN'T CHANGE PRIVACY SETTINGS If you share a photo or an album from a friend's page, the people you share it with may not see it because sharing does not change the privacy settings that the owner set up when the photo was posted.

If you want to share an entire album with your friends, follow these steps:

1. Find an album you want to share and click it.

2. In the bottom left of the album, click Share This Album. A pop-up display appears where you can enter specific friends' names and attach a message.

3. After entering this information, click Send Message to share the album with your selected friends.

4. You can also select to Post to Profile instead, and the To: line disappears and is replaced with an option to enter thoughts about the album and then Share it with all your Facebook friends, as shown in Figure 6-7.

SHARE WITH PEOPLE WHO DON'T USE FACEBOOK A cool functionality for albums that you create is the ability to share that album with non-Facebook users. At the bottom of your album page, you see a long URL that you can copy into an email or other sharing medium and send to people not on Facebook. Keep in mind this link works even if you add photos or change privacy settings for the album.

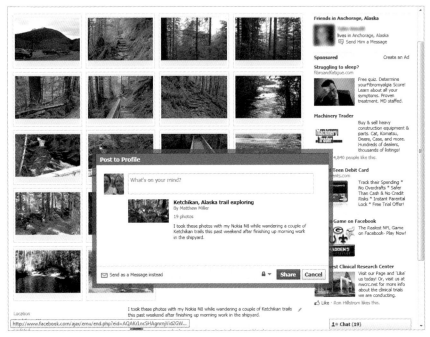

FIGURE 6-7 Post an album to your Profile

EDIT AND TAG PHOTOS

While the Facebook Photo Viewer could never be considered a photo editing program, you can take some basic actions. These include minor photo editing and photo tagging.

Minor Photo Editing

Photo editing in Facebook is limited to adding and revising a photo description, rotating the photo right or left, and changing the order in which the photos appear in an album. You cannot edit any image attributes in Facebook or even crop a photo (unless it is a profile picture, which the following section discusses). The Rotate buttons are found in the bottom right of the photo viewer, and the description editor is located directly under the center of the photo.

To reorder the images within your album follow these steps:

1. Go to the album you want to reorder.

2. Mouse over the photo you want to move, and notice the four-direction arrow in the upper left.

3. Click and hold on this arrow; then drag the photo where you want it placed.

4. The new photo order is saved automatically and reflected in both the album view and Photo Viewer.

Photo Tagging

Part of the benefit of having photos in a social network as large as Facebook is the ability to connect photos with people. If you see yourself or someone you know in a photo that is not tagged, you might want to consider tagging yourself or your friend. You can tag only your Facebook friends, but you can tag any photo you can view. You and your friend always have the ability to remove the tag if you do not want to be tagged in the photo. You can also set up your notifications so that you always know if you have been tagged.

LIMITED TAG REMOVAL POLICY The owner of the photo and the person tagged have the ability to remove a photo tag. Therefore, if you tag a friend in a photo you don't own, you do not have the ability to remove that tag; it moves to the tagged friend's or the photo owner's control.

To tag a photo, follow these steps:

1. Find a photo you want to tag, and click it to open the Photo Viewer.

2. In the bottom left of the view, click Tag Photo, or further down in the left menu, click Tag This Photo.

3. A target then appears on the display with the direction to click a person's face to tag them, as shown in Figure 6-8. Click the person you want to tag.

4. A drop-down of your friends appears. Start typing a name, and when the name you want appears, click it.

5. The photo is now tagged with your friend and will appear in his profile. The five most recently tagged photos appear in his new profile filmstrip at the top of his profile. You can tag up to 50 people in a single photo.

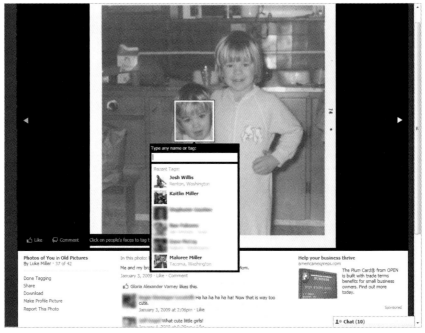

FIGURE 6-8 Tagging people in a photo

TAGGING NON-FACEBOOK USERS You can tag people who are not on Facebook by entering their email address in the text box in which you would normally put their name. They will then be sent a link to the photo and can see the photos they are tagged in but cannot do anything else on Facebook until they register for an account.

CHANGE YOUR PROFILE PICTURE

As mentioned in Chapter 2 (How Do I Set Up My Profile?), your profile picture is important because it is what people see on your Facebook page and in status updates you post; it even appears as your contact photo through many smartphone applications. Thus, you should try to have a profile picture that you like, and at times, may want to change or update it.

As pointed out earlier, Facebook creates a Profile Pictures album by default. You can visit this album and easily change your profile picture back to a previous one, or choose a new one.

To change your profile picture, follow these steps:

1. Click your Profile page; then click View My Profile.

2. Click Profile Picture in the left menu.

3. You can select to either choose a file on your computer or take a picture with your webcam to serve as your profile picture. After performing one of these selections, your new profile picture will be set.

- -

SHORT CUT FOR UPLOADING A PROFILE PIC From your main Profile page you can hover your cursor over your profile picture and choose the option to Change Picture right there; you'll jump right to step 2 from the previous list.

- -

You also have the option to edit the thumbnail that simply enables you to drag the thumbnail box around a bit within the frame of the allowed space, similar to cropping the photo. There is also the option to remove your picture, but it helps to have a photo associated with your account for quick recognition of you by others on Facebook.

Another method to change your profile picture, and one you might use because there are many more photos to choose from, is to select a photo you have already uploaded separately or in an album as your profile picture. To use this method, follow these steps:

1. Find a photo you like in your photo library, and open it up.

2. In the bottom-left menu, click Make Profile Picture.

3. The photo appears on a new page with a box indicating the size of the profile picture area. Drag the corners of the transparent box to crop the photo as your profile picture. Some pictures may not have this cropping option if they are already an appropriate size.

4. Click Done Cropping when you are happy with the editing, and the image then appears as your new profile picture.

Sharing Videos

Photos are quick and easy to share with your Facebook friends, but it is also fun to capture live action via video to share. Facebook enables you to upload videos recorded from your phone, camera, or webcam, which is great because it is often difficult to describe events via just text and photos.

- -

CAN I UPLOAD A YOUTUBE VIDEO? Although it is handy to have the ability to upload videos directly from within Facebook, a huge number of videos on YouTube are fun to share with others. You can share videos on YouTube and elsewhere directly from these other sites or you can do so by attaching a URL from external sites in the Share area. When you add these external links, a thumbnail (often selectable), appears in your Wall post.

- -

Facebook has an extensive list of supported video types, including the following:

- 3g2 (Mobile Video)
- 3gp (Mobile Video)
- 3gpp (Mobile Video)
- asf (Windows Media Video)
- avi (AVI Video)
- dat (MPEG Video)
- divx (DIVX Video)
- dv (DV Video)
- f4v (Flash Video)
- flv (Flash Video)
- m2ts (M2TS Video)
- m4v (MPEG-4 Video)
- mkv (Matroska Format)
- mod (MOD Video)
- mov (QuickTime Movie)

- mp4 (MPEG-4 Video)
- mpe (MPEG Video)
- mpeg (MPEG Video)
- mpeg4 (MPEG-4 Video)
- mpg (MPEG Video)
- mts (AVCHD Video)
- nsv (Nullsoft Video)
- ogm (Ogg Media Format)
- ogv (Ogg Video Format)
- qt (QuickTime Movie)
- tod (TOD Video)
- ts (MPEG Transport Stream)
- vob (DVD Video)
- wmv (Windows Media Video)

Although an extensive list of upload formats are supported, there are limits to which Facebook videos you can actually view and play if you are accessing Facebook from your smartphone. Refer to Chapter 10 (What are Facebook Places and Why Would I Want to Share My Location?) for more specific details on smartphone usage.

UPLOAD A VIDEO FROM YOUR DRIVE

Video uploading is similar to photo uploading, and the functionality is located in the same center Share area on your Facebook page. To upload a video from your computer, follow these steps:

1. On your main Facebook home page or Profile page, click the Video icon/link in the Share area on the far right of the display. Two video options appear after clicking Video as shown in Figure 6-9. Choose Upload a Video from your drive.

2. Click the Browse or Choose File button, as shown in Figure 6-10. A file explorer interface appears. Navigate to the video you want to upload, and double click it or click Open to select the video.

3. Enter text in the box that states, "Say something about this video...."

4. Click Share to post your video. A pop-up window appears with a status bar showing the upload progression.

5. After the video uploads, you can click Close and Edit Video or Close. If you click Close and Edit Video for more options, an Edit Video page opens. Here you can tag friends, enter a title and description, and set the privacy for the video. Click Save to save the edits.

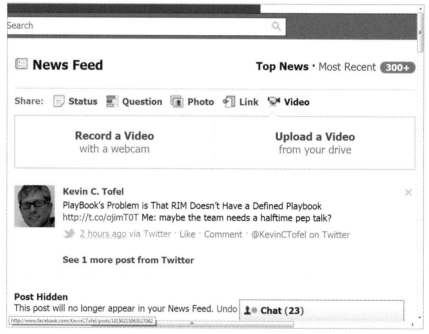

FIGURE 6-9 Video sharing options

FIGURE 6-10 Video file upload page

VIDEO UPLOAD LIMITS Facebook limits your uploaded video to 1,024MB and 20 minutes, so keep this in mind when you record a video that you plan to upload to Facebook. You may have to edit your video with a third-party program to get it to fit within these parameters.

After completing these steps, you may still see that the video is processing because a video takes time to process on Facebook's servers. You can click the check box to be notified when the video is done processing.

RECORD A VIDEO WITH A WEBCAM

You may also want to record and upload a video captured with your computer webcam. To upload a video that you record with your webcam, follow these steps:

1. On your main Facebook home page or Profile page, click the Video icon/link in the Share area in the far right of the display, and choose Record a Video with a webcam.

2. Click the red Record button in the video viewfinder. A 20-minute timer appears in the upper right and starts counting down. Record the content you want.

3. Click the button to stop the recording. Use the Play and Reset buttons in the lower-right corner to view your video or reset it and record another.

4. Enter text in the box that states, "Say something about this video...."

5. Click Share to post your video. A pop-up window appears with a status bar showing the upload progression.

6. After the video is uploaded, you can click Close and Edit Video or Close. If you click Close and Edit Video for more options, an Edit Video page opens up. Here you can tag friends, enter a title and description, and set the privacy for the video. Click Save to save the edits.

DO I NEED ADOBE FLASH PLAYER TO RECORD A VIDEO? Yes, the webcam functionality in Facebook is provided as a Flash plug-in, so you need the latest Adobe Flash Player to use your webcam. The first time you use the webcam, you will be prompted for this, and your computer connects to Adobe to check your client. Check the box to make sure you will not see this pop-up appear next time.

To view the videos after you upload, go to the Photos section of your Facebook page. In the upper right you see the quick link to your videos. Your video page, as shown in Figure 6-11, shows your videos, length of your videos, when you uploaded the video, the description, and any people tagged in your videos. You can choose to edit your videos (tags and description) and view the comments on your videos.

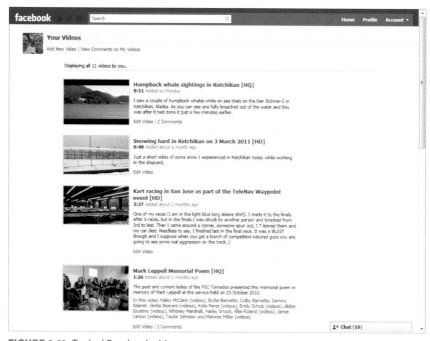

FIGURE 6-11 Typical Facebook video page

SEND A VIDEO IN A MESSAGE

Similar to the way you can send photos to your friends in a message, you can also share videos with friends privately. You can record a video or share videos already in your video library via messages, as described in the next section.

To include a new video that is not already on Facebook in a private message to a specific person(s), follow these steps:

1. Compose a new message to a friend; see Chapter 5 (How Do I Communicate With Friends?) for detailed steps on how to create messages.

2. In the New Message pop-up window, click the Camera icon and then the video camera icon (Switch to Video) to launch the video recorder (see Figure 6-12).

3. Click the red Record button and record a video.

4. Click the button to stop the video recording.

5. Enter some text to go with the video message.

6. Click Send to send the message to your friend.

Videos sent via messaging are also limited to 20 minutes.

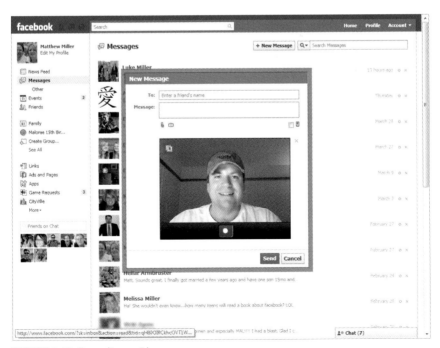

FIGURE 6-12 Recording a video message

SHARE VIDEOS WITH OTHERS

Although Photos has a new Photo Viewer interface, you will find the older interface in the video application. The primary difference between these interfaces is the pop out nature of the displays.

To share a video with others, follow these steps:

1. Find a video you want to share, and click it.

2. In the bottom right of the video page, click Share.

3. Enter a thought about the video, and click Share to post it to your Profile, as shown in Figure 6-13.

4. You can also click the bottom left to turn this sharing into a message, as detailed in the previous section.

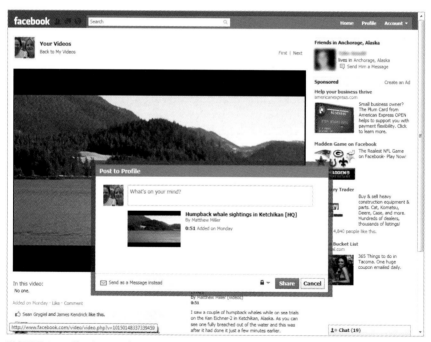

FIGURE 6-13 Sharing a video to your Profile

TAG AND COMMENT ON VIDEOS

As you can also see when you visit a video's Facebook page, you can Like/ Unlike, comment on, and tag people in the video. The Like/Unlike and Comment options are directly under the video.

You can tag people in the video by clicking the Tag This Video option in the lower right of the video's page, as shown in Figure 6-14. Unlike photos where you place the target over the person's face, in video tagging you simply enter the names of those in the video and then click the Done Tagging button to finish tagging the video.

You can comment only on your videos, your friends' videos, or videos in which you or your friends are tagged.

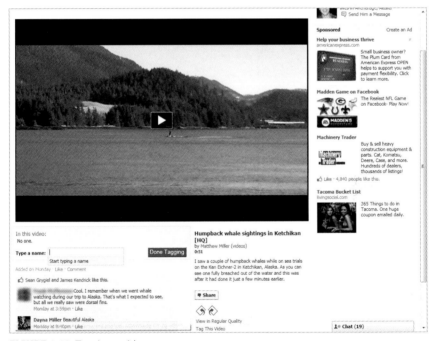

FIGURE 6-14 Tagging a video

CAN I TAG NON-FACEBOOK USERS IN VIDEOS? No, unlike photos, you cannot tag non-Facebook users in videos on Facebook.

Related Questions

✦ How can I create a message to my friend? **PAGE 57**

✦ How can I upload photos and videos from my iPhone or Android smartphone? **PAGE 126**

✦ How can I customize the privacy settings for my photos and videos? **PAGE 111**

CHAPTER SEVEN

WHAT ARE EVENTS AND HOW CAN I USE THEM?

In this chapter:

+ How Are Facebook Events Different Than My Calendar?
+ Create an Event and Invite People to Come
+ Manage Your Event
+ RSVP to an Event
+ Add Photos and Videos to an Event
+ Facebook Treats a Birthday as an Event

ince the Facebook platform is quite comprehensive, rather than having to send out physical invites or set up an event through a third-party
company, you can simply create a Facebook Event for upcoming gatherings
with your family and friends. You can include maps, links to more information,
and all the details for the event in one place. People can easily respond to the
invite, post comments, and share links, photos, and videos before and after
the event. Facebook turns your event into a community site that can provide
much more than a simple written invitation.

How Are Facebook Events Different Than My Calendar?

Even though the Events icon is a calendar and events are tied to specific days,
you cannot use the Events feature as your personal calendar; it's strictly an
event planning application. To access your events, click the Events link in the
left menu from your Home page. As you see in Figure 7-1, Events appear in a
chronological list in the center column of your Facebook page.

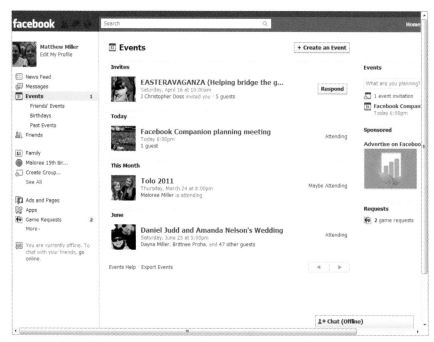

FIGURE 7-1 Typical Events page

SMARTPHONE SYNCRONIZATION Chapter 9 (How Can I Use Facebook Effectively on My Mobile Phone?) discusses how some smartphone programs label the synchronization with Facebook Events as Facebook Calendar, but don't be confused; it essentially is just syncing up your events and not creating or replacing a true calendar.

Even though you can't use Facebook Events as your sole calendar, you can export your Facebook Events into personal calendar programs such as Microsoft Outlook, Apple iCal, and Google Calendar. You can choose to only export a single event by clicking the URL at the bottom of the specific event page in question, but it is more efficient to export all your current and future events at once so you don't have to export each one individually. The following steps detail how to export all your Facebook Events to Google Calendar:

1. In the left column of your Facebook page, click Events.

2. At the bottom of the center column, click Export Events. A pop-up appears with a URL that looks something like this: `webcal://www.facebook.com/ical/u.php?uid=123456789&key=1x2x3x45xx` (see Figure 7-2).

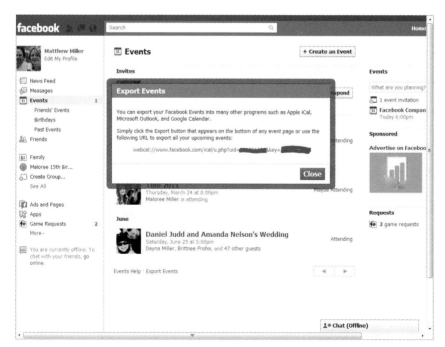

FIGURE 7-2 Exports Events pop-up

3. Copy the URL to your computer clipboard.

4. Log into Google Calendar, and choose Add under Other calendars. Then choose Add by URL (see Figure 7-3).

5. Paste the URL you copied from Facebook, and click Add.

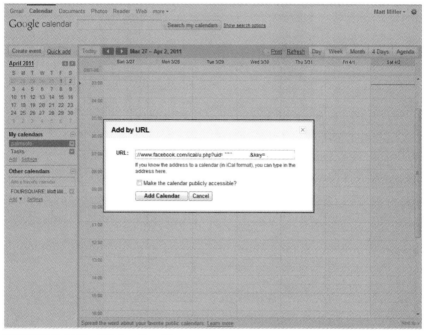

FIGURE 7-3 Add by URL functionality

You can then see the events you accept or decline appear or disappear from your Google Calendar. You can use this same copy URL method with other Calendar programs as well.

EXPORT MAY HAPPEN AUTOMATICALLY Depending on the type of computer you have (PC or Mac) and the type of calendar software you have loaded on it, you may be able to click directly on the pop-up URL and see specific events placed into your calendar automatically.

Create an Event and Invite People to Come

Now that you understand Facebook Events is primarily for advertising, managing, and sharing an event, take a look at how to create one and get people to join you. Events are subject to privacy settings, so you can create a public event or a private event. The following explains these events in greater detail.

- **Public Events:** These are created as an open invitation so that anyone can add themselves to the guest list without receiving an invitation. The event information and all shared content are visible to anyone, and the event shows up in searches. Companies often set these up when holding special events that are open to the public.

- **Private Events:** These are viewable only by the administrator and those who have been invited, regardless of whether they respond to come to the event. This event will show up on your profile for others to see, but if you were not invited, you cannot view the event's Wall, photos, videos, or other details, and you cannot see any feed stories about the event. (My family uses private events to plan birthday parties and other large gatherings.)

To create any of these types of events, follow these steps:

1. Look at the right column on your Facebook Home page to find the Events section. Put your cursor in the text box that says, "What's the event?" You see options appear for day, time, where, and who's invited, as shown in Figure 7-4.

2. Enter a title, date, time, and location for your event.

3. Enter names of Facebook friends who are invited. As you enter characters your Facebook Friends list filters through your friends and a drop down list of friends from which to choose. Click the names of the friends you want to invite.

4. Click the Lock icon on the right to select whether it is a public or private event.

5. Click the Create Event button to create the event and have invitations sent out.

FIGURE 7-4 Create an event from the right-column creator

You may find you want to add more details than what is available in this quick event creator. To add more details, click the Add Details hyperlink. When you click this, another page opens up, as shown in Figure 7-5, with the following options:

+ Add an end time (usually a good idea for most events).

+ Add an event photo (used as the thumbnail for the event).

+ Enter a specific street address, so a map can be automatically embedded.

+ Select guests from your Facebook friends with a quick selector that appears as a pop-up when you click the Select Guests to Invite button.

+ Toggle whether guests can invite their friends (ones that are not in your Facebook friends list).

+ Toggle whether to show the guest list on the event page.

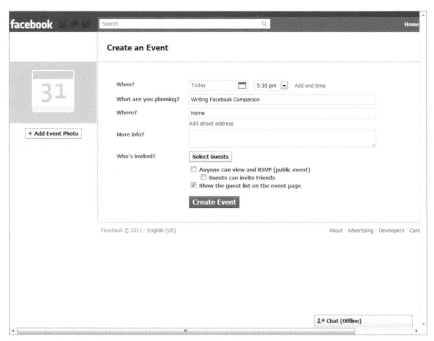

FIGURE 7-5 Adding details to an event

It is best to add all these details before sending out the invites to the guests because this type of information should limit questions.

INVITE OTHERS WHO ARE NOT FACEBOOK USERS Similar to the way you can share photos with non-Facebook users, you can also invite them to events by entering an email address. The invitee can view the event information and RSVP but cannot view any other Facebook information or interact with other guests through Facebook.

ARE THERE LIMITS TO THE NUMBER OF PEOPLE I INVITE? You can invite an unlimited number of people to your Facebook event, but you can send invites only in groups of 100. You can also have only 300 pending invites at one time, so if you have more than this, people need to respond to clear the queue.

Manage Your Event

Now that you have an event created and invitations sent, you just have to wait for people to RSVP and be ready to respond to any of their questions. There may be times when you need to change the date or time, remove a guest invitation, change the location, or perform some other management of the event, which can all be performed easily via the Edit Event function.

To edit your event, simply do the following:

1. Navigate to the event's page from either the right column of your Home page or the main Events page.

2. Click the upper-right Edit Event button that looks like a pencil.

3. The detailed event entry screen appears, as described earlier. Make any changes and then click Save Event. Notifications will also be automatically sent if you decide to make changes to your event. In the bottom-right corner of this Edit Event screen, you can also find the option to Cancel this event, which simply removes it from Facebook.

CANCELLATIONS WILL BE SENT If you decide to cancel an event, after selecting to cancel it, you see a pop-up appear where you have the option to add a personal note about the cancellation before Facebook sends an email to everyone canceling the event. This also gives you a chance to change your mind.

You may also decide to co-host an event or designate others to help you manage it and serve as the admin. To designate another Facebook friend as an admin, follow these steps:

1. Click the event and the event page opens up.

2. Look in the left column for the friend you want to set as an admin, and click the word View (or See All if there is a list of more than one person) to the right of their name. A pop-up box appears.

3. Note their attendance status; then look to the far right of this new pop-up box. Click Make Admin to give that friend the same access you have to this particular Event.

Removing administrative access is the same process with a different final button to click.

1. Simply follow the preceding steps 1-3;

2. When the final pop-up box appears, click Remove Admin. Alternatively, you can click the X to remove them from the guest list completely. People you remove from admin or the guest list will not receive a notification that they have been removed, but they will not have the same editing privileges or the event will not appear on their Upcoming Events list.

- -

WHERE IS THE OPTION TO CHANGE MY EVENT NAME? You can change the name on the edit page only if you do so before people confirm their attendance. After an event has confirmed guests, the name is set and cannot be changed.

- -

RSVP to an Event

You should receive an email invitation (if you enabled this setting) in addition to a Facebook notification when someone invites you to an event. The email contains hyperlinked buttons that let you choose from one of these options:

- Attending
- Maybe Attending
- Not Attending

You can respond right there in the email by clicking one of the hyperlinked options. If you want to see more details before you respond though, log into Facebook and navigate to the main Events page from the left column on your home page. On the right side of the center column you can indicate your response to all events to which you are invited. Alternatively, go to the specific event's page and use the upper-right buttons on the event's page to choose your response status.

When life throws unexpected curve balls your way, you may need to change your response status for an event. To do so follow these steps:

1. Navigate to the main Events page from the left column on your Facebook Home page or use the See All link in the right Events column of your Home page.

2. Click your current status to the right of the event's name.

3. Select a different status in the pop-up box that appears, as shown in Figure 7-6. Click the RSVP button to confirm your change.

Alternatively, you can perform Step 3 from the specific event's page by clicking your status at the top of the page by the event's name. Figure 7-6 displays a user accessing the RSVP pop-up box using this method.

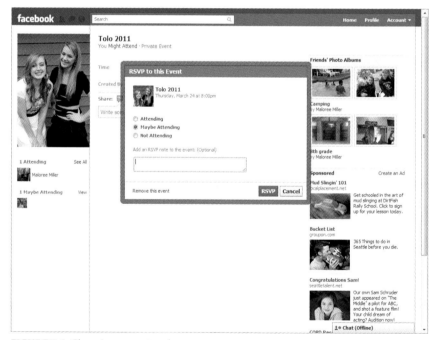

FIGURE 7-6 Changing your attendance status

You may also be interested in seeing what other guests have responded. To do so, look in the left column and you can see the status for those attending, maybe attending, awaiting reply, and not attending, as shown in Figure 7-7. Note that these are friends of the event admin and are not necessarily just your friends. You can also look to the top center column of the event's page to see if this is a public or private event.

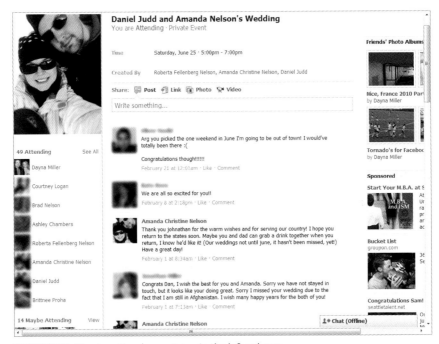

FIGURE 7-7 Viewing attendance status in the left column

WHAT ARE FRIENDS' EVENTS? When you click Events in the left column of your Home page, you see a subdirectory appear with Friends' Events. If you click this, you can see all the public events your friends are attending. Click them to see if you are interested in joining your friend for an outing.

If you receive invitations you don't want to see on your page, you can simply click the X that appears when you hover over the event. There is also a Remove this Event button on the top of the event's page that will do the same.

Add Photos and Videos to an Event

Events that are created appear almost as an entirely different page of your Facebook account. An event page has the ability for people to interact with it similar to the way they do with you, including making Wall posts, sharing hyperlinks, and posting photos and videos. The photo and video upload functionality is the same as that detailed in Chapter 6 (How Do I Share Photos and Videos?), except that you cannot create an album with many photos on an event page.

As mentioned earlier in this chapter, you can upload a photo for an event that serves as the event photo, similar to your profile picture. Photos and videos can be uploaded from your drive or taken with a webcam, and the same functions and limitations detailed in Chapter 6 apply.

To add photos or videos to an event, follow these steps:

1. Navigate to the event page and, similar to the way you interact with friends on their Wall, click on the Photo or Video link in the center column on the Share line.

2. Choose to upload a photo or video or capture one with your webcam.

3. Perform your chosen action and click to Share the photo or video.

Keep in mind that event admins have the ability to remove photos or videos they do not want associated with their event so you can rest easy knowing you have full control over what appears on your event page.

Facebook Treats a Birthday as an Event

Facebook places an emphasis on birthdays, and if you look in the left column of your Facebook home page, you can see Birthdays appear as a subcategory under Events. If you click this Birthdays link, you see a list of upcoming birthdays, and depending on privacy settings, you may even see how old that person is going to be, as shown in Figure 7-8. This is a great way to keep track of friends' birthdays so you can write on their wall to wish them a happy birthday!

There are multiple ways to see which of your friends have upcoming birthdays in addition to viewing the Birthdays subcategory of Events. These include:

+ In the right column of your Home page, Facebook lists the friends who have birthdays that day under Upcoming Events.

+ On the day of your birthday, Facebook lists at the top of your Profile page "Today is his/her birthday."

+ On the main Events page (pictured in Figure 7-1) Facebook includes upcoming friends' birthdays in the general listing of upcoming Events.

+ If you subscribe to Facebook birthday notifications (found under the Notifications tab in My Account) Facebook sends you a weekly email with a brief summary of all your friends who have birthdays that week. You can unsubscribe from these weekly notifications right from the email by clicking unsubscribe at the bottom of the message.

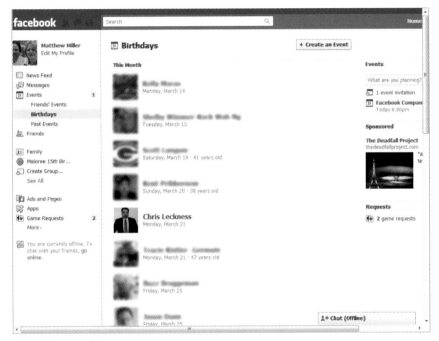

FIGURE 7-8 Birthdays

Birthday notifications are set up by default on Facebook, but you can also control what notifications you receive from friends and who, if anyone, sees your own birthday. You can choose to hide your birthday in your privacy settings, but then you will miss out on all the great birthday wishes and comments from your friends on your special day. If you hide your birthday completely, then your Facebook Friends won't receive any reminders or notifications informing them of your big day. To manage what your Facebook friends see regarding your birthday, you can follow these steps:

1. Navigate to the Edit Profile page and note the menu options in the left column. Click on the Basic Information option in the left menu.

2. On your birthday line, look over to the right and click the drop down box. Note these three choices:

   + Show my full birthday in my profile.

   + Show only month and day in my profile.

   + Don't show my birthday in my profile.

3. Select one of the choices and then click the Save Changes button to save them and have your chosen birthday setting accepted.

Just as you did with Events, you can also choose to export birthdays to your calendar. Follow the instructions in the section "How are Facebook Events Different Than My Calendar?" to learn to do so, but start from the Birthday's page instead of the Event's page. Many smartphone clients also pull in your friends' birthdays when they sync to the calendar functionality of Facebook.

Related Questions

+ What are the specific steps to share photos and videos? **PAGES 68 AND 82**

+ Can I tie Events in with my business to promote or sponsor something? **PAGE 226**

CHAPTER EIGHT

HOW DO I OPTIMIZE MY PRIVACY SETTINGS?

In this chapter:

+ Privacy Settings
+ Account Security
+ Report Abuse
+ Deactivating, Deleting, and Memorializing Accounts

Although social networks can be a great way to share information, communicate with friends, play games, use applications, and learn more about people and companies, you also need to know they are a safe place to be. Privacy and security are important to Facebook and you can manage a variety of custom settings to maintain a level of privacy you are comfortable with and keep your account information secure. Due to the nature of the type of information shared on Facebook, you need to visit this area of your account and take the time to make sure your settings are optimized for your needs, rather than just accepting the defaults that may change from time to time.

Privacy Settings

Facebook establishes and implements default or recommended privacy settings for every new account, which, if left untouched, enable everyone to find you in a search. The amount of information people see on your profile when they click your name from a search is by default your name, gender, profile picture, username, and networks. For most people, the default level of these settings is not quite adequate, and even if it is, the default settings change occasionally, so you must visit the privacy settings area of your account to make sure your information is properly protected.

- -

CAN I UPDATE MY ACCOUNT SECURITY QUESTION? No, after you have added a security question to your account, then that security question cannot be changed.

- -

Facebook has a detailed privacy policy that covers the information they receive and how they use and protect it. It also outlines how to change or remove your information and cautions you on sharing information on Facebook. Read it at www.facebook.com/policy.php before putting too much up on Facebook.

To access your Facebook privacy settings, follow these steps:

1. Log in to your Facebook account.

2. In the top-right corner, select the arrow next to Account and choose Privacy Settings from the drop-down menu.

You can now see four main areas available for you to access and customize, as shown in Figure 8-1.

+ Connecting on Facebook

+ Sharing on Facebook

+ Apps and Websites

+ Block Lists

The Controlling How You Share link at the bottom right of this page reveals more about each of these four privacy areas in detail.

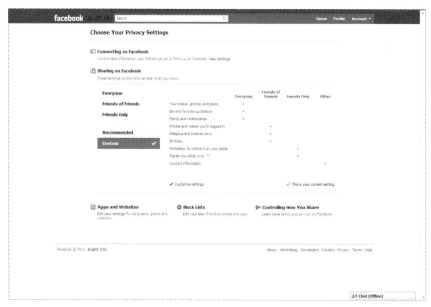

FIGURE 8-1 Privacy Settings main page

The chart in the middle of the page shows your current settings. You can change these settings for each area by clicking the hyperlinks. These hyperlinks vary for each section. They include:

+ View Settings under Connecting Facebook

+ Customize Settings under Sharing on Facebook

+ Edit Your Settings under Apps and Websites
+ Edit Your Lists under Block Lists

With the exception of Edit Your Lists under Block Lists, each of these links takes you to a list of Facebook functions for which you can set various privacy levels. Examples of these functions include, send messages, see friends, and see education and work history (these functions are discussed in further detail in the following sections). After clicking one of these links, you can click the lock icon to the right of each function to choose your desired level of privacy. A few options are available to establish these levels of privacy settings:

+ **Everyone** is anyone on Facebook, friend or not.
+ **Friends of Friends** refer to anyone who is friends with a friend of yours.
+ **Friends Only** are simply the confirmed friends in your Facebook network.
+ **Custom** gives you the option to customize your settings outside of the three preceding categories.

These are the four main privacy levels and therefore the ones listed on your main Privacy page. Some functions only give you a few of these options, and some give you an extra option: Networks. Networks include all the people in the network(s) to which you belong, friends or not. The Networks privacy option may also come paired with one of the four main options.

If you want to create Custom settings, select the Customize link and you see the pop-up as shown in Figure 8-2. From the Make This Visible To drop-down box, select one of these options:

+ Friends of Friends
+ Friends Only
+ Specific People (then use a contact/people picker)
+ Only Me

You also notice a bottom section to choose to Hide This From, so you can prevent specific people from seeing your posts or other selected updates.

The following sections discuss each of these Privacy areas in detail.

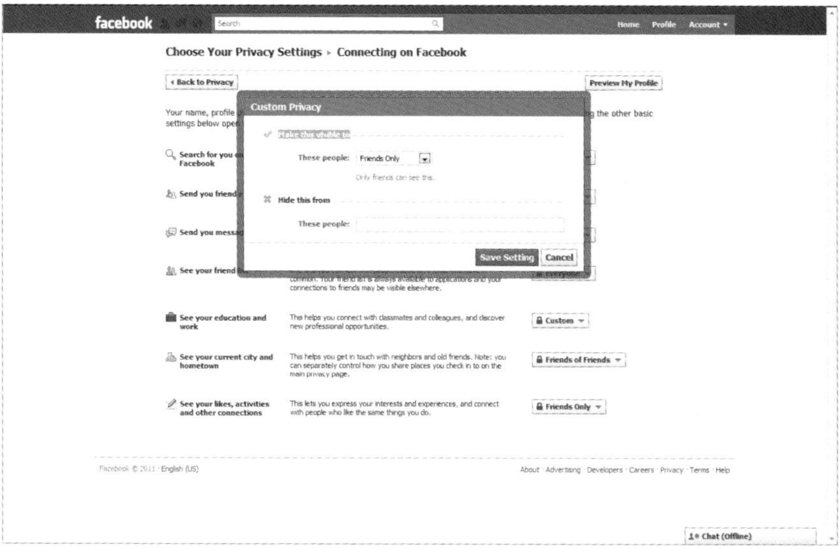

FIGURE 8-2 Customize pop-up dialog box

CONNECTING ON FACEBOOK

The first section where you control privacy settings is at the top of the page called Connecting on Facebook. Facebook's definition of this category reads, "Control basic information your friends will use to find you on Facebook." Click View Settings to see more options for controlling this information (see Figure 8-3). Another page appears with the following options on the left side:

+ Search for you on Facebook

+ Send you friend requests

+ Send you messages

+ See your friend list

+ See your education and work

+ See your current city and hometown
+ See your likes, activities, and other connections

Each of these options has a drop-down box where you can choose to allow access to one of the privacy levels discussed previously. As you can see in Figure 8-3, these settings help you customize your profile page sharing options. Choose the options best for you and click Back to Privacy.

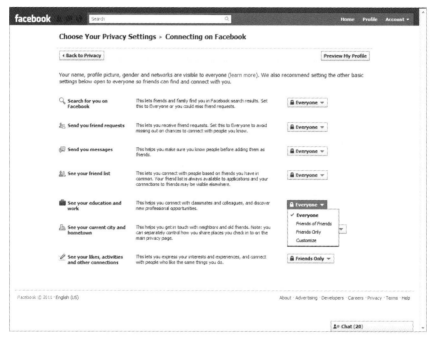

FIGURE 8-3 Connecting on Facebook Privacy Settings

HOW CAN I CHECK MY PUBLIC PROFILE? After you make changes to your privacy settings, you may like to see what your public profile will look like with the changes. Simply look to the upper right on the Connecting on Facebook settings page to find the Preview My Profile button. Click it to check out what most people see when they see your profile, and click the Back to Privacy Settings button to return when you finish viewing it.

By default, all these items previously listed are set to Everyone because Facebook wants to make it easy for friends to find and connect with you. This default setting has angered some Facebook users who failed to customize their privacy options. Make sure to check the description of each option, and select the privacy setting that satisfies you.

- -

REMEMBER: FACEBOOK PROTECTS EVERYONE'S PRIVACY, NOT JUST YOURS You always have the ability on your end to limit visibility of your information so you can control who has access to your information. On the other hand, Facebook limits your ability to track things such as who viewed your profile, who viewed your photos, and how often a particular Wall post you made is viewed by others as a means to protect your friends' privacy and allow them to view content without hesitation.

- -

SHARING ON FACEBOOK

The Sharing on Facebook section is the main section of your privacy settings and controls who can see what you share. Down the left side of this center area are the words Everyone, Friends of Friends, Friends Only, Recommended, and Custom. Click each one of them to see how the settings for the categories of information on the right change. The categories of information you can share include the following:

+ Your status, photos, and posts
+ Bio and favorite quotations
+ Family and relationships
+ Photos and videos you are tagged in
+ Religious and political views
+ Birthday
+ Permission to comment on your posts
+ Places you check in to
+ Contact information

You also see an option to Customize settings, and if you select this hyper-link, you see a page appear with a more detailed breakdown of the things you share, things others share, and contact information (see Figure 8-4). Many smartphones enable you to access and use the contact data stored on Facebook, so make sure you know what details are being shared with others. You may want to share your cell number but not your home number, which is one of the functions you can set from this section.

FIGURE 8-4 Customize page for sharing settings

The best way to modify the settings to your specific tastes is to select this option to customize the settings and meticulously go through the list of func-tions for which you can set privacy levels.

APPS AND WEBSITES

On the bottom left of the Privacy Settings page, you see an Apps and Websites label. To access these settings, click Edit Your Settings. A page appears, as shown in Figure 8-5, with access to the settings for the following:

+ Apps you use

+ Info accessible through your friends

+ Game and app activity

+ Instant personalization

+ Public search

FIGURE 8-5 Apps, Games, and Websites settings

Each function except for games and app activity has buttons labeled Edit Settings. Clicking the button for each one of these options presents you with a different user interface and options to customize the specific settings.

- -

WHAT IS THE X TO THE RIGHT OF EDIT SETTINGS IN THE APPS YOU USE CATEGORY FOR? Facebook enables you to manage your installed status for your applications in the Privacy Settings area. To remove an application, click the X and a pop-up a confirmation box appears so you can verify this is the action you want to take before removing an application.

- -

You can edit the settings for each application or service that you use through Facebook. You might find that some apps have required settings and optional ones, so if you do not like the required setting, you should remove the application for your Facebook account.

BLOCK LISTS

At the center bottom of the Privacy Settings page, you see the words Block Lists. Select Edit Your Lists to bring up the page for monitoring your block lists. You see the following sections:

- Block users
- Block app invites
- Block event invites
- Blocked apps (only appears if you have at least one app blocked)

Here, if perhaps someone is harassing you or you don't want your boss to see your profile, you can enter a name or email to block a person and then select Block This User.

Here you can also choose to keep from getting invites to games and apps you never play or use by entering the name of a friend who keeps sending you these invites.

- -

WHAT HAPPENS WHEN I BLOCK INVITES? You will automatically be ignored for future app requests and events from the friend that you blocked.

- -

Blocked apps appear in the bottom center, and after you block them, the apps can no longer contact you or use your information. You can unblock apps and then participate as intended if you change your mind.

Account Security

As Facebook continues to grow its user base at a fast pace, the number of scammers increases. It is important to make sure that you do not click suspicious links, do not leave your account logged in on a public computer, ensure you have a strong password, and make sure not to share your account login details with anyone. Spam can appear in fake emails, within groups, within pages, or within events, so use caution when browsing Facebook, and try to only click links from sites with which you are personally familiar.

To take extra precautions against hackers, it is a good idea to set up secure browsing and login alerts from your account settings so that you can monitor the computer used to log in to your account. Do so by following these steps:

1. Log in to your Facebook account.

2. In the upper right, select the arrow next to Account and choose Account Settings.

3. In the Settings tab, look down to Account Security, and click Change. Options below this line expand and reveal check boxes for secure https browsing and new device login alerts, as shown in Figure 8-6. If you accessed Facebook from devices other than your computer then you will see them listed.

4. Check the boxes you want to set up for your account security.

You can view the devices that were used to access your Facebook account, and if any are not legitimate, you can click to remove them. You can also view your most recent account activity to see through what method your account has been accessed.

If you do suspect that your account has been compromised, Facebook has methods to secure your account and assist you with resolving the issues, so contact Facebook as soon as you suspect something suspicious is going on with your account.

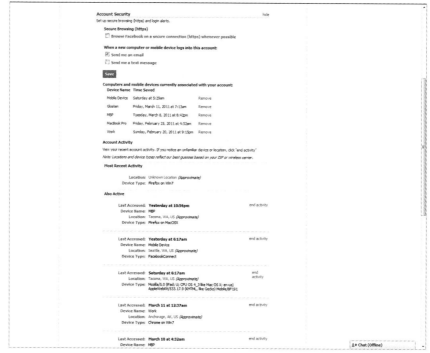

FIGURE 8-6 Account security settings

Report Abuse

Facebook has Report links throughout the site, so if you ever run into inappropriate or illegal content, click the link and fill out the requested information, as shown in Figure 8-7. You can file reports for the following:

+ Profiles

+ Photos

+ Inbox Message

+ Groups or Events

+ Pages

If you find something and report it, you may also want to think about blocking the person that had the content posted. This will not affect the report in any way.

FIGURE 8-7 Filling out a report form for an inappropriate photo

Ensure your facts are correct before you report someone or something because after it has been submitted, there is no way to retract the report. The Facebook administrators research and review every report before taking action. One possible outcome of abuse of Facebook is banning that person from Facebook and having their account deleted.

Deactivating, Deleting, and Memorializing Accounts

You can remove yourself from Facebook in two ways: deactivation and deletion. Deactivation makes your profile and information inaccessible to your Facebook friends, but your information is still saved by Facebook, and you can reactivate when you feel like returning. This may be good for people traveling on extended trips, experiencing extended illnesses or hospitalization periods, or just wanting to take a break from Facebook for some time.

To deactivate your account, follow these steps:

1. Log in to your Facebook account.
2. In the upper right, select the arrow next to Account and choose Account Settings.
3. In the Settings tab, look down to the option to Deactivate Account and click the right link to deactivate.

You can also delete your account, and if you choose this method all your information will be purged from Facebook's database. To delete your account, you need to visit the Help section of the site and find the link to the form to request an account deletion. The Facebook system delays the deletion process in case you change your mind. After an account is deleted, there is no way to undo the action.

If one of your friends who has an account passes away, you can report their death to Facebook. To do so, fill out the Report a Deceased Person's Profile report found at `www.facebook.com/help/contact.php?show_form=deceased` and as shown in Figure 8-8.

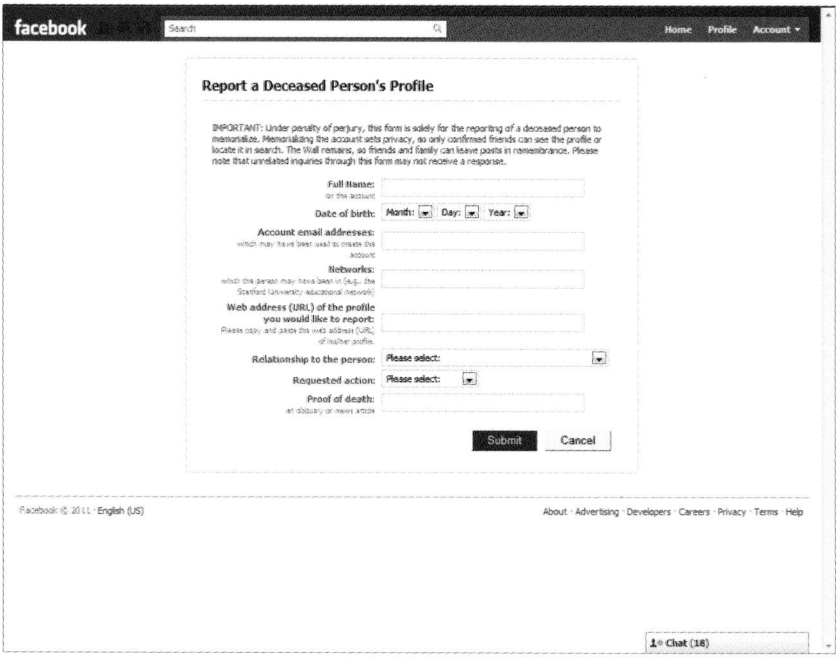

FIGURE 8-8 Report a Deceased Person's Profile report page

When Facebook receives a report that a member has passed away, it memorializes the account by setting the account privacy so that only confirmed friends can see the profile or locate it in a search. The Wall remains intact so that family and friends can leave posts. No one is allowed to log in to accounts of deceased members.

Close family members may also request to have the account closed completely and deleted from the Facebook servers.

Related Questions

+ How can I customize my profile? **PAGE 12**
+ Is it safe to share my location? **PAGE 161**
+ Where can I find apps to install? **PAGE 180**

CHAPTER NINE

HOW CAN I USE FACEBOOK EFFECTIVELY ON MY MOBILE PHONE?

In this chapter:

+ Facebook Mobile Texts
+ Facebook Mobile Web
+ Upload Photos From Your Mobile Phone
+ Facebook Smartphone Applications

A fter you get hooked on Facebook, you may discover that you can't get enough and want to take it on the go with you. Because of modern technology, you can do so with nearly any mobile phone. Today's advanced smartphones even offer experiences that many find richer than the full Facebook website accessed via a computer at your home or office. Facebook and third-party developers give you plenty of options for updating your status, checking on your friends' status, sharing photos and videos, checking in to various virtual locations, and much more. This chapter starts with the basic cell phones and moves up to the higher-end smartphones. If you have a smartphone, feel free to jump ahead to discover how you can use Facebook on the go.

Facebook Mobile Texts

As a father of three daughters, I cannot afford to have the entire family setup with smartphones and expensive data plans. Therefore, my oldest daughter, a major Facebook fan, accesses Facebook regularly via a standard mobile phone that has no data plan thanks to Facebook Mobile Texts.

The first step to use Facebook Mobile Texts is to activate it through the full Facebook website from a computer. Follow these steps to get your mobile phone set up for your account:

1. Log in to your Facebook page.

2. In the upper right, select the arrow next to Account and choose Account Settings.

3. Select the Mobile tab (the fourth tab from the left).

4. Select Register for Facebook Text Messages and then follow the Setup Wizard that includes entering your phone number and selecting your mobile phone carrier.

5. After receiving the confirmation code text message, enter it into the appropriate area and select to confirm. You are now set up for text messaging.

Make sure to then look through the rest of the settings in the Facebook Text Messages area that enable you to customize your experience (see Figure 9-1). Settings for Facebook Text Messages include the following:

✦ Select the notifications that will appear on your phone (sending you a message, pokes, birthdays, and many more available options).

✦ Toggle on or off to get text notifications only from your friends.

✦ Choose the time of day when text messages should be sent to your phone.

✦ Limit the number of daily texts.

✦ Toggle for confirmation texts.

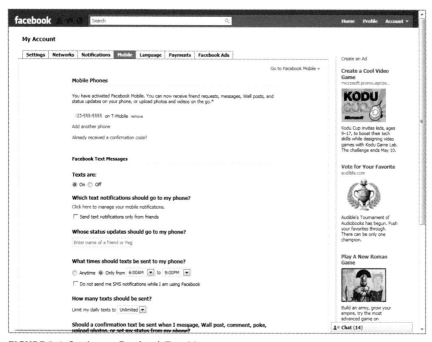

FIGURE 9-1 Setting up Facebook Text Messages

MY CARRIER ISN'T IN THE DROP-DOWN LIST OF CARRIERS
Unfortunately, your carrier must be supported and in the carrier selection drop-down list or you cannot use Facebook Text Messages. Facebook does have a form for carrier suggestions, so fill that out if your carrier is not supported.

Facebook does not charge you anything extra for this access, but standard text messaging rates apply from your carrier. The following Facebook functions are supported through Facebook Text Messages:

- Update your status
- Send Facebook messages
- Receive Facebook messages
- Receive a friend's status updates
- Search for a friend
- Retrieve a friend's phone number
- Check on Events
- Post to your Wall
- Add a friend by name or phone number

CAN I UNSUBSCRIBE OR STOP TEXT MESSAGES FROM FACEBOOK? Yes; you can simply text **Off** in reply to the last message Facebook sent you to disable Facebook Text Messages right from your phone. You can also disable your text message notifications from your Facebook page on a computer.

As you can see there are actually several Facebook functions that you can perform simply through text messaging. All this interaction is via your phone's text messaging client though, and as a text-based experience it's not nearly as feature-rich as what you can expect using Facebook Mobile Web or a smartphone application.

Facebook Mobile Web

To access the Facebook Mobile Web you need data on your phone and a basic Internet web browser. After you have a working data package, follow these two steps:

1. From your web browser, go to m.facebook.com or touch.facebook.com if you have a touchscreen mobile phone (see Figure 9-2).

2. Enter your email or phone number and password to access the site. To save some time, make sure to add this mobile Facebook site to your bookmarks or favorites for future access.

FIGURE 9-2 Facebook Mobile Web

IS THERE A CHARGE FOR FACEBOOK MOBILE WEB? Facebook does not charge you to access this mobile site on your phone. However, standard data rates will apply from your carrier. Make sure you know if there are any data limits on your plan before you blow through your allotment checking Facebook on the go.

After visiting the Facebook Mobile Web page, you can find that the site supports the following features:

+ Posting on your Wall
+ Commenting on a friend's post
+ Poking your friend
+ Viewing and responding to Event invites

+ Finding and adding friends

+ Viewing your groups

+ Managing your notifications

+ Viewing messages

+ Uploading photos

+ Editing privacy settings

As you can see you actually have access to nearly all the most common functions of Facebook right from within your phone's web browser (see Figure 9-3). Features such as Facebook Chat and viewing videos are not supported, but if you upgrade to a smartphone you will find that advanced functions are supported.

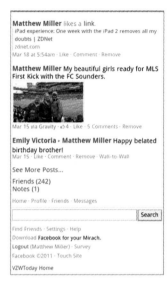

FIGURE 9-3 Common Facebook functions available via the mobile website

---

Upload Photos From Your Mobile Phone

There are several ways to upload photos from your mobile phone: You can upload via email, as described in Chapter 6 (How Do I Share Photos and Videos?). You can text in a photo to your Facebook page, as noted in the section on Facebook Mobile Texts. You can also upload photos straight from your data-enabled mobile phone.

To upload photos from your phone through the Facebook Mobile Web interface, perform the following steps:

1. Select the Photos hyperlink found on Facebook Mobile Web.

2. Select the Upload Photos link and you will see the screen displayed in Figure 9-4.

3. Click the Choose File or Browse button. A pop-up or another display appears that enables you select a photo from your phone to upload.

4. After selecting the photo, enter a photo caption in the text box on the website.

5. Click the Upload button to upload the photo to your Facebook page (see Figure 9-5).

FIGURE 9-4 Upload photos from the mobile website

FIGURE 9-5 Uploaded photo can now be tagged

CAN I DOWNLOAD PHOTOS FROM MY FRIEND'S ALBUM? No, there are privacy settings on the mobile clients that do not allow you to download photos from your friends. You can view, comment on, and Like their photos though.

Facebook Smartphone Applications

Smartphones are growing in popularity thanks to the great consumer user experiences found on platforms such as Apple's iOS and Google Android. Facebook is accessible on all these platforms and some, such as Windows Phone 7, can integrate Facebook support into the mobile operating system. Others incorporate Facebook via a third-party application, some of which actually surpass the ease of using Facebook on the computer.

APPLE IOS DEVICES

Apple set the bar for smartphone user experience in late 2007, and the Facebook application for iOS devices (iPhone and iPod touch) continues to be one of the best mobile applications available. The Apple iPad also runs iOS, but as of this writing there isn't a native Facebook application for this device.

Facebook Home on Apple iOS

To access Facebook on your iOS device, go to the App store and download the Facebook App. When you launch it, you see the Facebook home screen that has nine icons for the main functions, shown in Figure 9-6, which are the following:

- + News Feed
- + Profile
- + Friends
- + Messages
- + Places
- + Groups
- + Events
- + Photos
- + Chat

FIGURE 9-6 Apple iOS Facebook app home screen

Although these are the same nine icons on Android devices, slide from right to left to see an additional screen on iOS (see Figure 9-7). Here you can find an icon for Notes with a lot of empty space.

The great thing about iOS is that you can fill this empty space with your favorite friends (also shown in Figure 9-7). To do so, follow these steps:

1. On the Favorites page, tap the upper-right + sign.

2. Find a friend or a page that you want to set as your favorite and tap on your chosen selection. A thumbnail of your favorite appears on the Facebook home screen.

FIGURE 9-7 Additional home screen for notes and favorites

YOU ARE IN CONTROL You can also move around your favorites and even the nine default icons. Similar to how you move application icons on iOS devices, tap and hold on the icons and then simply drag them where you want them to stay. Tap Done in the upper-right corner when you are satisfied with their placement.

There are two additional active areas on the Facebook home screen:

+ **Account**: Tap this button in the upper left to find options to log out, access account settings, access privacy settings, view the help center, and cancel your action (see Figure 9-8).

+ **Notifications**: Tap this area at the bottom of the screen to bring up your most recent notification; then tap on that to take action, as shown in Figure 9-9.

FIGURE 9-8 Account button options   **FIGURE 9-9** Recent notifications

---

TAP FACEBOOK TO JUMP TO THE HOME SCREEN As you navigate around Facebook on iOS and dive into different functions, remember that you can always tap on the word Facebook centered on the display to return to the main home screen.

Perform Common Facebook Tasks with Your iOS Device

One of the most common tasks you will likely perform with your Facebook application is to post a status update. To do so, follow these steps:

1. Tap the Profile icon, and then tap inside the text box with the grayed out text What's on Your Mind? You can also tap News Feed and then tap the Status button to do the same.

2. Enter your status update into the text box that pops up (see Figure 9-10).

3. You can also include a photo or video from your gallery or capture one with the camera by tapping the Camera icon to the left of the What's on Your Mind? box.

4. Tap Share to update your status.

FIGURE 9-10 Status entry pop-up

- -

UPLOAD VIDEO The iOS platform is one of the only platforms that enable you to upload video content on Facebook.

- -

You will also likely want to interact with friends on your new Facebook application. To post on your friend's Wall, follow these steps:

1. Tap Friends from the home screen or tap the Search icon in the upper right to quickly filter your friends list and find your friend.

2. After you find your friend, tap her name to open up her profile page. You can view her Wall (the default landing page), Info, and Photos (see Figure 9-11).

3. Enter something in the text box on the Wall tab, over the grayed-out words Write Something, to add a comment to her Wall. Alternatively, you can upload a photo or video to her Wall. You can also tap the + icon next to one of her Wall posts and leave a comment in the pop-up box.

4. Tap on Share to post your comment, photo, or video.

In addition to support for video posting, iOS stands out from most other mobile clients with the capability to interact with your Groups (see Figure 9-12). Remember that you can create private groups where you can share comments and photos within a select group of individuals. To interact with one of your Groups, follow these steps:

1. Tap on the Groups icon from the home screen.

2. Tap on a Group you want to interact with.

3. Tap on one of the two top buttons to either write a post or share a photo (from your gallery or capture a new one).

4. Tap Share or Upload to post your content to the Group.

FIGURE 9-11 Viewing your friend's profile page

FIGURE 9-12 Accessing your Groups

You can also comment on and Like existing posts within your Group from this same interface.

Facebook on iOS is also one of the only mobile clients you can use to engage in Facebook Chat. To do so, follow these steps:

1. Tap the Chat icon from the home screen.

2. Tap on the upper-right button, Go Online, to see your friends' statuses. A list of your friends appears with either green icons (ready to chat) or blue partial moons (idle) showing their availability status, as shown in Figure 9-13.

3. Tap on a friend to open up a chat window and then enter text that you want to send.

4. Tap Send after entering your text. You can also view your friends' profiles in the chat window if you like.

5. Carry out a conversation in the threaded message view of Facebook Chat on iOS.

You can tap the upper-right button and change it to Go Offline when you finish chatting with your friends.

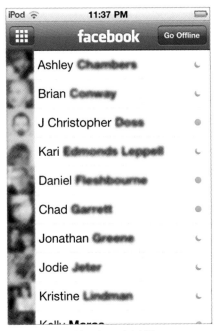

FIGURE 9-13 Chatting with iOS

GOOGLE ANDROID DEVICES

Although Facebook is not baked into the Android operating system by Google, different phone manufacturers have integrated Facebook support into user interfaces and applications that they preload onto their devices. For example, HTC includes Facebook support in its HTC Sense user interface, so Facebook appears there and through the official or third-party Facebook application.

Facebook Home on Android

You can download the Facebook native application for free from the Android Market, which was updated in March 2011 to nearly match the experience provided on iOS devices (see Figure 9-14).

The Facebook for Android application has a "home" screen with the following icons in a 3x3 navigation grid (same as iOS):

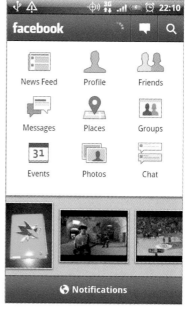

- News Feed
- Profile
- Friends
- Messages
- Places
- Groups
- Events
- Photos
- Chat

FIGURE 9-14 Android Facebook home screen

In addition to these nine icons, the home screen contains three additional parts:

- At the top of the main screen, the icons on the right help you quickly post your status update or search for friends in Facebook.

- Along the bottom of the main screen, you see a photos filmstrip with the latest photos appearing in your Facebook feed.

- At the bottom of the display is the Notifications area, and like the main Android notifications area, this can be pulled up or slid down like a reverse window shade.

Perform Common Facebook Tasks with Your Android Device

Now take a look at a few of the basic functions you will likely want to perform on your Android device. You can tap on the home screen icons to discover the rest when you have some time.

To post a status update on your Wall, follow these steps:

1. Tap the conversation icon in the upper right of your display. A screen appears with the cursor placed inside a text box with the grayed-out words What's on Your Mind?

2. Enter your status update, as shown in Figure 9-15. You can also choose to include a photo from your gallery or capture one with the camera by tapping the Camera icon to the left of the text entry box.

3. Tap on Share to update your status.

FIGURE 9-15 Entering your status update

- -

HOW DO I GET BACK TO THE ANDROID FACEBOOK HOME SCREEN?
As you move around in the Facebook Android application, you may find yourself deep into the application. Simply tap the Facebook icon in the upper left to jump back to the home screen.

- -

To post on your friend's Wall, follow these steps:

1. Tap on Friends from the home screen, or tap on the Search icon in the upper right to quickly filter your friends list and find your friend.

2. After you find your friend, tap on his name to open up his profile page. You can view his Wall (the default landing page), Info, and Photos, as shown in Figure 9-16.

3. Enter something in the text box on the Wall tab to post a comment to his Wall. You can also choose to open up something on his Wall and leave your own comment at the bottom of the screen.

4. Tap on Share to post your comment.

FIGURE 9-16 Viewing your friend's wall

Nearly all Android devices come with cameras and some are quite good. Android has a well-integrated sharing support, so you can post photos to your Facebook page from the photo gallery app. You can also post from within Facebook by following these steps:

1. Tap on the Photos icon from the home screen.

2. Tap on the Camera icon in the upper right of the display.

3. Choose to upload from the Gallery or capture a photo from the camera, as shown in Figure 9-17.

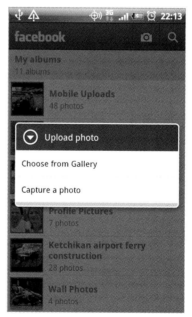

FIGURE 9-17 Uploading a photo to share

4. Add a caption to the photo.

5. Tap the Upload button to share your photo on your Facebook page.

NO VIDEO UPLOAD WITH ANDROID CLIENT At the time of this writing, unlike iOS, the Android client does not enable you to upload videos and is limited to photo sharing only.

You can also easily view and comment on the most recent photos from your friends by simply tapping on a photo in the bottom filmstrip and then leaving comments or choosing to Like a photo.

RIM BLACKBERRY DEVICES

You can find the official Facebook for BlackBerry application in the BlackBerry App World software store on your RIM BlackBerry device, but that version is quickly becoming outdated. As of April 2011, Facebook 2.0 is available to install through the BlackBerry Beta Zone and includes Facebook Chat, a new UI, profile info, and enhanced news feeds. RIM is set to release this updated version in May 2011 to the App World Store.

Facebook Home on Blackberry

Facebook 2.0 software has a look and feel that is similar to the latest iOS and Android versions with a home screen that includes the navigation grid with the following icons:

- News Feed
- Profile
- Notifications
- Search
- Messages
- Friends
- Chat
- Places
- Photos

Figure 9-18 displays the home screen. You also notice there are two drop-down areas in the upper bar whose functions follows:

+ The drop-down area on the left matches the navigation grid icons, so you can navigate through Facebook in a couple of different ways.

+ The drop-down on the right is called the Notifications Bar, and it shows you your notification status for friend requests, messages, general notifications, and chat conversations. This is similar to what you see on the website; when you have a new notification, a red highlight appears on the Notification icon.

FIGURE 9-18 BlackBerry Facebook 2.0 home screen

While you are checking out your friends' feeds, note the + icon on the right. If you select this, you see a pop-up appear with the following options:

+ Comment

+ See Wall to Wall

+ Switch application

+ Home

+ Like

+ Full menu

Simply select one of these options to take the action described.

Perform Common Facebook Tasks with Your Blackberry Device

Like iOS and Android, Blackberry enables you to perform almost all the common tasks you would do on the regular Facebook website. To post a status update on your Wall, follow these steps:

1. Select the News Feed icon in the navigation grid, or select it from the drop-down box on the left. A screen appears with the cursor placed

inside a text box with the grayed-out words What's on Your Mind? (see Figure 9-19).

2. Enter the text of your status update. You can also choose to include a photo from your gallery or capture one with the camera by selecting the Camera icon to the left of the text entry box. You can also select the Places icon to the right to share your location with your status update.

3. When you finish entering text and making your Photos or Places selection, activate the Share button to update your status.

One of the major improvements in Facebook 2.0 for Blackberry is the support for Facebook Chat on the BlackBerry platform, with a significant change in the user interface. Chat on a BlackBerry appears similar to the website with the familiar green Circle icon appearing when your friends are online and available to chat. To chat with friends, follow these steps:

1. Select the Chat icon on the navigation grid or from the drop-down list. This logs you into Facebook Chat and shows which friends are also currently logged in to Facebook Chat, plus any open conversations you have (see Figure 9-20).

2. Select a friend from the list (who has a green circle indicating

FIGURE 9-19 News Feed in Facebook 2.0

FIGURE 9-20 Facebook Chat launched on a BlackBerry

availability) and you see a chat window open up with your friend's name, photo, and status.

3. Enter text into the open text box, and press return to send your message.

The Facebook for BlackBerry 2.0 application shows your chats in a functional threaded conversation view as shown in Figure 9-21, so you can easily keep track of who said what. Notice that there is also a + icon in the top status bar, so you can access the BlackBerry menu items listed earlier in this section.

Another major improvement in Facebook 2.0 for the BlackBerry is the ability to view your friend's profile, including the Wall, info, and photos, as shown in Figure 9-22.

FIGURE 9-21 Chatting with a friend on a BlackBerry

FIGURE 9-22 Viewing a friend's profile page

MICROSOFT WINDOWS PHONE 7 DEVICES

Microsoft directly integrated some Facebook functionality in its Windows Phone 7 operating system. You can check out the book *Windows Phone 7 Companion* for all the details on the Facebook integration, but the following is a brief look at what is integrated. There is also an official Facebook application for Windows Phone 7, covered in this section as well.

Integrated Facebook on Windows Phone 7

One of the account setup options in Windows Phone 7 is Facebook, and by simply entering in the email address and password you used to set up your Facebook account, you can find your contacts, photos, and feeds integrated into the device. There is a toggle setting for your contacts, so you can show all your Facebook friends in your contact list or just have Facebook information for your existing contacts appear on your Windows Phone 7 device.

Following are some of the great things you can do on Facebook via the integrated Windows Phone 7 device:

✛ When you view the contact information for one of your contacts, slide from right to left to see her latest Facebook feed. From here you can read, like, and comment on her Wall.

✛ View all your contacts' latest status updates by selecting the general People hub rather than a specific contact's detail page.

✛ In the Pictures hub you can see your Facebook friends' feeds filtered just to show you the latest photos that were posted. You can view them and also comment on them.

✛ View your own Facebook photos in folders in your Pictures hub. Photos you capture with your Windows Phone 7 device can be set to upload automatically to your Facebook account without you needing to do anything other than capture the photo.

Facebook Home on Windows Phone 7

You can download the official Facebook for Windows Phone 7 application from the Windows Phone Marketplace for free. This application has a similar user interface to iOS, Android, and BlackBerry, but the navigation grid appears as a navigation list with the following shortcuts (see Figure 9-23):

FIGURE 9-23 Windows Phone 7 Facebook home screen

+ News Feed
+ Photos
+ Messages
+ Places
+ Events
+ Friends
+ Profile
+ Requests
+ Notes
+ Settings
+ Logout

CAN I CHAT ON WINDOWS PHONE 7? As of the writing of this book, Facebook Chat is not supported in Windows Phone 7.

If you slide from right to left (this is the Metro user interface) you can find Top News, Photos, Events, and then Notifications on different pages, so you can quickly slide around to see some of your latest Facebook information.

Perform Common Facebook Tasks with Your Windows Phone 7

Much like the previously devices, to post something on your own Wall, simply follow these steps:

1. From the Facebook home screen, tap on the top where your Facebook profile photo displays.

2. Tap into the text entry box where the words What's on Your Mind? appear (see Figure 9-24).

3. Enter text into the text box. You can also tap on the Camera icon to select a photo in your gallery or capture a photo to share.

4. After you enter some text and select a photo, tap the Post icon at the bottom of the screen to post to your Wall.

You can also find the + icon throughout the Facebook for Windows Phone 7 application. Tapping this opens up the specific post, photo, or status update and then gives you the opportunity to write a comment and Like the post that you are viewing.

If you select one of your friends, a page opens that enables you to slide left or right to view his Wall, info, albums, photos of him, and his pages. From within this specific friend area, you can also send him a private message or poke him using menu options on the bottom of the display.

FIGURE 9-24 Preparing to enter a Wall post

HP WEBOS DEVICES

Palm's webOS, now owned and branded by HP, is an attractive, modern, and functional operating system. Similar to what Microsoft did with Windows Phone 7, HP integrates some features of Facebook into its HP Synergy system and also enables the Facebook application.

Integrated Facebook on HP webOS

With the integrated HP Synergy support and the Facebook for webOS application installed, you can perform the following Facebook functions:

+ View Facebook info in the Contacts app

+ Use the Photos app of webOS to upload photos directly to Facebook

+ Send status updates using the Just Type utility of webOS 2.0

Facebook Home on HP webOS

You can also access the full Facebook application on your HP webOS device. The version available as of April 2011 is 1.5. The primary new feature included in this version offers support for Facebook Places. You can also perform the following functions with the Facebook for webOS application:

- Post status updates
- Upload and tag photos
- Read your News Feed
- Browse your friends' photo albums and profiles
- View videos posted on Facebook (one of the first mobile operating systems to support this)
- View upcoming Events
- Access notifications

The interface for the latest Facebook for webOS application is similar to the ones for iOS and Android, with fewer functions. You can find that familiar navigation grid on webOS, but it includes seven icons instead of the nine found on other smartphone platforms. These seven icons, as shown in Figure 9-25, follow:

- News
- Photos
- Search
- Inbox
- Profile
- Events
- Places

FIGURE 9-25 webOS Facebook home screen

SHAKE TO RELOAD Within the Preferences & Accounts section of the webOS Facebook application you can choose to enable Shake to Reload so you can simply shake your smartphone to refresh your Facebook feeds.

Similar to how the Facebook website has a top blue bar, the webOS client also has this design element. There are three main elements of the upper blue bar, as shown in Figure 9-26 and described in detail here:

✦ **Left Globe icon:** Tapping on this icon brings up your most recent Facebook notifications. You can tap on these to go to the person or activity listed in the notification. You also see red numbers added on top of the Globe icon as unread notifications appear on your device. The number resets to zero after you tap the Globe icon to view your notifications.

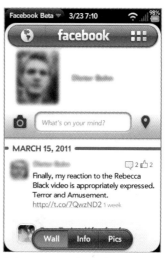

FIGURE 9-26 Three elements of the Facebook upper blue bar

✦ **Center Facebook text:** Tapping on the word Facebook brings you back to your News Feed if you are anywhere else within the application. If you are already on your News Feed page, tapping this word takes you to the top of your feed, and tapping again takes you to the bottom.

✦ **Right Grid icon:** The Grid icon located on the right brings up the page with the seven icons mentioned earlier in this section.

Perform Common Facebook Tasks with Your HP webOS phone

Much like the previous devices, to post something on your own Wall, simply follow these steps:

1. From the Facebook home screen, tap on the center icon labeled Profile.

2. Tap into the text entry box where the words What's on Your Mind? appear.

3. Enter text into the text box as shown in Figure 9-27.

4. After you enter some text, tap the Update button to post to your Wall.

The Facebook for webOS application is easy to use and understand because of the fluid operating system. Facebook Chat is supported in webOS 2.0 devices as well; but only with the HP Pre 3 and HP Veer smartphones, which are scheduled to launch later in 2011.

NOKIA SYMBIAN DEVICES

On February 11, 2011 Nokia announced a partnership with Microsoft to launch Nokia hardware running the Windows Phone 7 operating system. However, the millions of Nokia devices available today currently run the Symbian OS.

FIGURE 9-27 Preparing to enter a Wall post

Symbian^3 devices launched in late 2010. Like Windows Phone 7 and Blackberry, Nokia provides an integrated Nokia Social client (version 1.3 was available in April 2011) that supports Facebook and Twitter social networking services. Symbian^3 only supports Facebook from this integrated platform or through a browser-based version however, and you cannot find a Facebook application in the Ovi Store.

Facebook Home on Symbian

To access Facebook through Nokia Social on your Symbian device, follow these steps:

1. Tap the Nokia Social icon to launch the service.

2. Tap on the Facebook icon and enter your Facebook account login information (email and password). After you login the first time, your Symbian device should remember your login email and just prompt you for your password on future login sessions.

You are now at the main Facebook page in Nokia Social that shows your News Feed by default (see Figure 9-28). Five icons appear on the top, giving you quick access to the following functions (from left to right):

+ **Home:** Jump back to the Facebook News Feed display.

+ **Inbox**: View received and send new messages.

+ **Events**: View scheduled events.

+ **Friends**: Quickly access your friends' profile, send them a message, or call them.

+ **Notifications**: View friend requests, invites, and more that you receive through the Facebook service.

FIGURE 9-28 Main Facebook page in Nokia Social

CAN I SHOW SOMETHING ELSE ON MY HOME SCREEN? By default the News Feed is enabled as your homescreen, but a small arrow to the right above the News Feed content gives you the ability to view your News Feed, Pages, Status Updates, or Photos. Clicking this arrow doesn't permanently change the Home screen to what you choose though.

Perform Common Facebook Tasks with Your Symbian Device

On both the News Feed display and Notifications display, you can enter and post a status update in the What's on Your Mind? text entry box. To the right of this box is a Camera icon that enables you to share either a photo (from your gallery or capture one) or a video (see Figure 9-29 for details). When you open up a post from one of your friends, you have the typical Facebook options to leave a comment or Like the post (see Figure 9-30 for details).

The Symbian client is not as intuitive and full featured as the other smartphone platforms, but it is still much better than using the Facebook Mobile Web interface.

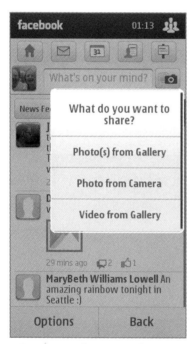

FIGURE 9-29 Choosing to share a photo or video

FIGURE 9-30 Available options when viewing a friend's Wall

Related Questions

✛ What are the specific steps to share photos and videos? **PAGES 68 AND 83**

✛ I see Places on my smartphone. What is that for? **PAGE 152**

✛ Which Facebook applications can I access on my smartphone? **PAGE 197**

CHAPTER TEN

WHAT IS FACEBOOK PLACES AND WHY WOULD I WANT TO SHARE MY LOCATION?

In this chapter:

+ What Is Places?
+ Share My Location with Places on a Mobile Phone
+ Create and Edit a Place
+ Tag Friends at a Place
+ Check Info and Add Photos for a Place
+ Receive Discounts for Using Places
+ Places Privacy

You may have heard of the Foursquare or Gowalla location-based applications that enable you to virtually check in to a location and earn badges and mayorships as a social networking gaming experience. Facebook also has Facebook Places to enable Facebook users to connect with friends in the real world rather than just through the Internet. Checking into Places is possible only through supported mobile devices (because you rarely physically go anywhere with your home computer). You can edit and manage the actual Places from your computer though. Places is designed for you to either share your location experience or help you connect with friends on the go.

What Is Places?

Places is a geo-location based service that enables you to check into a Place, tag your friends, and view comments that your friends make about a Place. This can be great for when you are trying to meet up with a group of friends or want to see what your friends thought about a restaurant you are visiting. Facebook created Places in an attempt to help friends connect face-to-face.

Share My Location with Places on a Mobile Phone

You need a mobile phone to check in to Places, but not necessarily a smartphone. Although many smartphones include a Places utility, (see Chapter 9, [How Can I Use Facebook Effectively on My Mobile Phone]) you can also use a mobile phone with a web browser to access Facebook and share your location through Places. To share your location with a feature phone browser, follow these steps:

1. Launch your phone web browser.
2. Visit `http://touch.facebook.com` (see Figure 10-1).
3. Tap on the Places tab.
4. Tap Check In to let your friends know where you are.

Sharing your location on a smartphone is quite similar. I used an Android smartphone for all the examples in this chapter, but you can perform the Places functions listed in this chapter with any smartphone that has a Places utility. To share your location on a smartphone, follow these steps:

1. Launch the Facebook app or third-party application that supports Facebook.

2. Look on your Facebook home screen for a Places icon within the application. Tap the icon to launch the Places utility. A list of your friends who have recently used Places appears.

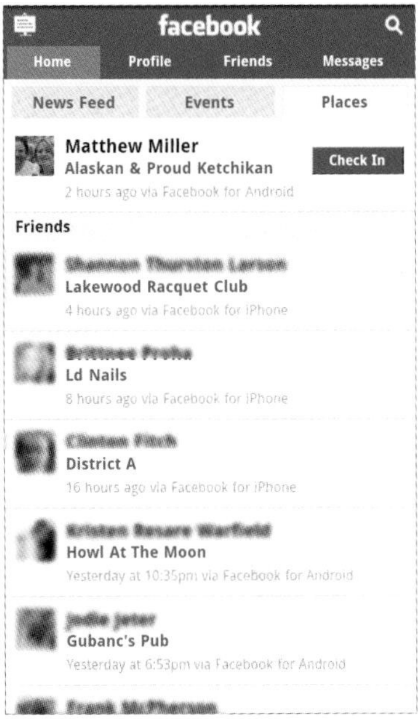

FIGURE 10-1 Accessing Places via the mobile web

3. Tap the Check In button on the display. Your phone determines your location and provides a list of places near you. Choose your location and tap Check In.

After you share your location from Places on your mobile phone, the information is uploaded to Facebook in the form of a status update on your wall. Each Place has its own Place page on Facebook and a hyperlink to this page is included in your Places status update. If you visit the Place on the Facebook site after checking in, you see that the Place page lists the number of check-ins, how many times you have checked in, and how many people like this Place. See Figure 10-2 for a typical Places page.

You can also see that a small map of the Place is inserted by default on the Place page, sponsored by Bing Maps. You can click on the map to open it up in a larger window and switch from road to aerial or even hybrid, as shown in Figure 10-3.

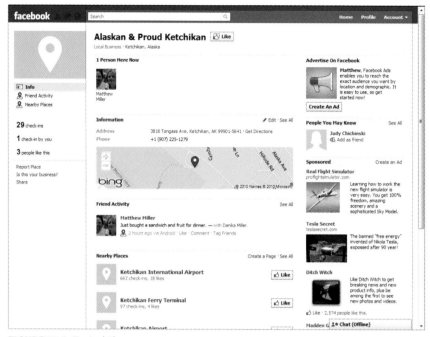

FIGURE 10-2 Typical Places page

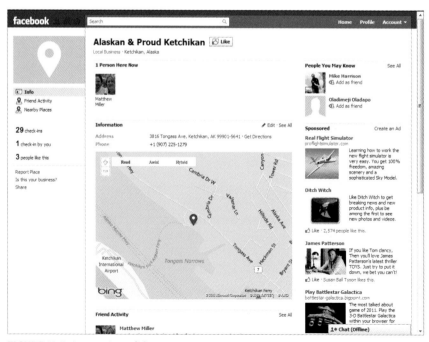

FIGURE 10-3 Larger view of the map

Create and Edit a Place

If a place that you are at doesn't already have a Facebook Place page, you can create one for it and add it to the database of Facebook Place pages. You can do this for either a public, well-known place that just happens to not have a page yet (for instance, your work) or you can create your own place (for instance, My House, or My Parent's House). To do so from your mobile phone, follow these steps:

1. From the main Facebook application launch page, tap on the Places icon. A list of your friends who have recently used Places appears.

2. Tap the Check In button on the display.

3. If you do not see your current location, start entering the name of your location to perform a search of nearby places. If this search does not turn up a positive result, tap Add "Name of your place." A map opens up with a text box for the name of your place and one for a description of the place (see Figure 10-4).

4. Fill these text boxes out and tap on Add to add the place to the Facebook Place network.

Sometimes, however, it is not that easy or convenient to enter in a Place name and description on the go from your phone. Therefore, you can go to the Facebook website when you get home and edit the Place page you added. Follow these steps to edit a Place:

1. Navigate to your Wall and find the status update noting the Place you checked into. Select the link to the Place you want to edit, and open up the Place page.

2. On the right of the center column across the Information line, find and then click Edit. The page changes to an editable page (see Figure 10-5).

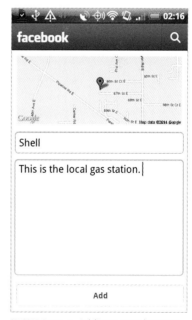

FIGURE 10-4 Adding a new location

3. Edit the category, name, address, phone number, website, or email.

4. Click the Save button to save the new details for the Place.

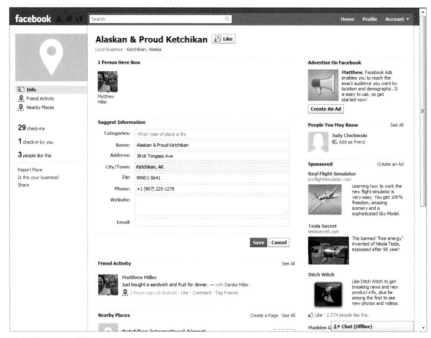

FIGURE 10-5 Editing Places

HOW IS THE PLACE SAVED ON FACEBOOK? If you click the link of the Place you created, you see that a Community Page is made for that Place so that others can see it and enhance the details of the Place as well.

Once you check into an existing Place, you cannot delete it from the Facebook database yourself. You can, however, flag or report a location from your smartphone (see Figure 10-6) or your computer and you will find the following options:

From your smartphone:

+ Incorrect info

+ Abusive

+ Permanently closed

+ Duplicate

From your web browser:

+ Spam or scam

+ Contains hate speech or attacks an individual

+ Violence, crime, or self harm

+ Nudity, pornography, or sexually explicit content

+ Inaccurate info

+ Other

FIGURE 10-6 Flagging options

Tag Friends at a Place

One of the reasons Facebook created Places is so that you can connect with your friends. The page of a Place shows you any friend activity at that Place and also enables you to view nearby Places. Click the nearby Places option to see a list of Places with stats on the number of check-ins and Likes for the Place.

- -

YOU CAN SHARE DETAILS ABOUT THE PLACE You can also click the Share link to write some other information about the place and share the Place with your Facebook friends. Then your post will have more details than just your basic Place status update.

- -

In a few of the mobile applications, you can simply use the feature in the application to tag friends that are with you. For example, on an Android device, follow these steps:

1. From the main Facebook application launch page, tap on the Places icon. A list of your friends who have recently used Places appears.

2. Tap the Check In button on the display.

3. Tap the button labeled Tag Friends With You as shown in Figure 10-7.

4. Choose the friends who are with you from your Facebook friends list and then tap the Done button.

5. Tap the Check In button.

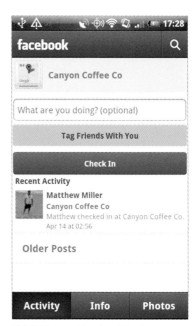

You can also visit the Facebook website to tag friends, using these steps:

1. Look in your profile for the Place you checked into.

2. After you find that Place, click the Tag Friends hyperlink.

3. Select the friends that were with you from the pop-up window. (You can also search for them if you have a lot of friends and do not want to scroll through lists.) See Figure 10-8 for the pop-up view.

FIGURE 10-7 Tagging friends on a smartphone

4. Click the Submit button to tag your friends as being with you at the Place.

Sometimes your friends may not want to be tagged at the Place. Similar to the way it works for photos, your friends can go in and remove their tags for Places. You can also choose to remove the story you posted for the Place, aka "checkout" of a Place if you decide you do not want to share those particular location details with your friends. To do so, simply click the X to the right of the status update and it disappears.

FIGURE 10-8 Tagging your friends in Places on the web

Check Info and Add Photos for a Place

In addition checking in to a location and tagging friends, you can also view Info and Photos for a location. Place Info is a great way to see an activity stream of other friends who visited that same Place in the past and a list of other friends who are checked in to the same Place at the same time as you. To view more information and photos for the location you are visiting, follow these steps:

1. From the main Facebook application launch page, tap on the Places icon. A list of your friends who have recently used Places appears.

2. Tap the Check In button on the display.

3. Tap your location. A page opens up with tabs for Activity, Info, and Photos as shown in Figure 10-9.

4. Tap on the Info tab to see the number of check-ins, location address, and the number of people that Like this location, as shown in Figure 10-10.

5. Tap on the Photos tab to view any photos people posted for your location.

FIGURE 10-9 Three available tabs when you check in

FIGURE 10-10 Info tab information in Places

You may also wish to post your own photos via the Places utility. To do so follow these steps:

1. From the main Facebook application launch page, tap on the Places icon. A list of your friends who have recently used Places appears.

2. Tap the Check In button on the upper right corner of the display.

3. Tap the Check In button on the Activity tab. You will see a button now appear labeled Add Photo. See Figure 10-11.

4. Tap the Add Photo button and then choose a photo from your Gallery or choose to capture a photo with your smartphone camera.

5. Add a caption to the photo and then tap the Upload button to attach the photo to the location.

FIGURE 10-11 Option to add a photo through Places

Receive Discounts for Using Places

One of the hopes and promises of these social location apps is the idea that users receive discounts or coupons for checking into a place on a regular basis or during a special occasion. While viewing nearby Places on your mobile device or web browser, you can see available check-in deals by looking for a yellow ticket next to a Place. These deals are not offered by Facebook but by individual businesses, and there may be limited quantities.

Facebook lists the following check-in deals for Places users:

+ **Individual deal:** Deals that merchants offer just to one individual when he checks in that is often used to clear out inventory or launch a new product.

+ **Friend deal:** Available for merchants to offer discounts to groups of up to eight people when they all check in together.

+ **Loyalty deal:** Awarded after a certain minimum number of check-ins are met; Facebook policy states that the deal must be offered after at least two check-ins and no more than twenty check-ins.

+ **Charity deal:** Can be created as a way to make donations to charities.

Check-in deals are a great way to generate excitement for businesses and also satisfy customers. Keep an eye on your smartphone for these deals as you use Places.

Places Privacy

Privacy on Places is easy to control because you have to physically and con-sciously decide to share your location and carry out all the actions to make this happen. Facebook will not share your location automatically.

If you do decide to use Places and check in from your phone, you can go into your privacy settings and manage the settings by taking these steps:

1. In the upper right of your Facebook page, select the arrow next to Account and choose Privacy Settings.

2. In the Sharing on Facebook section, find the line labeled Places You Check In To and see what is currently selected.

3. To change it click Customize settings, find the Places You Check In To line once again, and choose everyone, friend of friends, friends only, or other.

Additionally, within the Privacy Settings area, click Customize settings to discover a line labeled Include Me in People Here Now After I Check In with a toggle to enable or disable this feature, as shown in Figure 10-12.

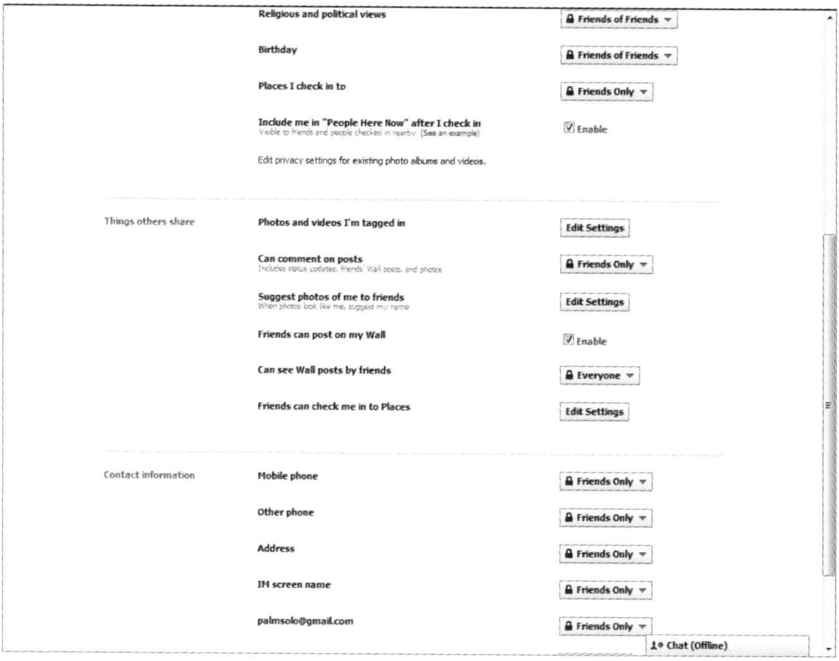

FIGURE 10-12 More privacy settings to check

Further down this same Customize settings page, you can find a line labeled Friends Can Check Me In To Places. Edit these settings to your liking as well. As you can see there are a few places to check to ensure your privacy is maintained to the level you want.

Related Questions

+ Where can I find my privacy settings? **PAGE 28**
+ How can I add more friends? **PAGE 44**
+ What smartphone apps support Places? **PAGE 128**

CHAPTER ELEVEN

WHAT ARE GROUPS AND HOW CAN I USE THEM?

Facebook is a great way to stay up to date with your friends, but it can be a bit overwhelming if you have a large number of them. To help you focus on specific groups of people, such as your immediate family, soccer team, or others that you really care about, Facebook created Groups. With Groups you can perform all the great Facebook functions while keeping posts, chats, information sharing, and discussions in a subset of your entire network of friends.

What Is a Group Used For?

Groups are used to communicate and share with a subset of your Facebook friends list without having to seek each one out individually. Figure 11-1 shows a typical group page. Although these same friends could see what you post in their feeds, setting up a Group helps filter Facebook feeds so that Group members know what you posted is meant for them specifically.

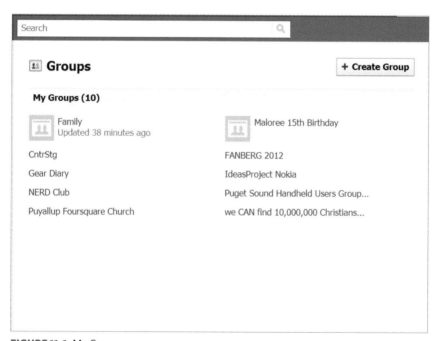

FIGURE 11-1 My Groups

Groups are great for having closed discussions; sharing private photos, bringing together individuals with common interests, and just maintaining a new level of privacy within a group of chosen individuals. There are many reasons to create or join a group. A few specific uses for groups follow:

+ **Family:** I have a Group set up for my immediate family members so we can share family inside jokes, goofy photos, and personal videos with one another that we wouldn't normally share with our entire Facebook friend network.

+ **Teams/Clubs**: A sports team is a great use of Groups for sharing team plays, practice times, and game schedules without having to alert all of Facebook.

+ **Projects:** Have a group project with classmates to whom you don't want to give your email? Create a Facebook group! You can share documents within your group or interact via Group chat, a feature that expands the instant messaging capability of Facebook.

+ **Common Interests**: Are you obsessed with Hello Kitty and want to meet fellow Hello Kitty lovers? Have you read every Dean Koontz book out there and want to discuss them with a group of people? Join a Facebook Group and chat away.

Create a Group

It is easy to create a new Group; you only need to make four decisions. The following list explains how to do so:

1. On your Facebook home page, click Create Group in the left column.

2. Click the arrow in the top left of the pop-up box. Here's where you make your four decisions:

   + Choose an icon to assign to your group, as shown in Figure 11-2. This icon appears next to your Group name in the left column of your Facebook page.

   + Come up with a Group name.

✦ Pick the friends you want in the group. As you type letters, your Facebook friends list is auto-filtered, so you can easily select your friends.

✦ Decide on the privacy settings you want for your group.

3. Click the Create button to create your new group.

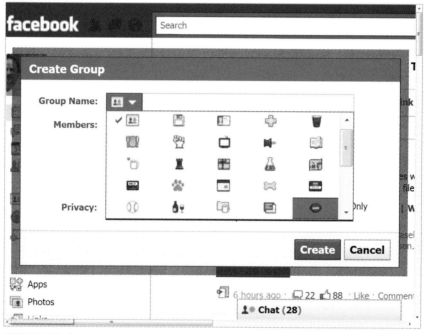

FIGURE 11-2 Group creation pop-up box

- -

CAN I DESIGNATE MORE GROUP ADMINS? The person who creates the group becomes the default admin. You can add more help by selecting to See All Group members and then clicking the Make Admin option under the names of those you want to serve as admins. See Figure 11-3.

- -

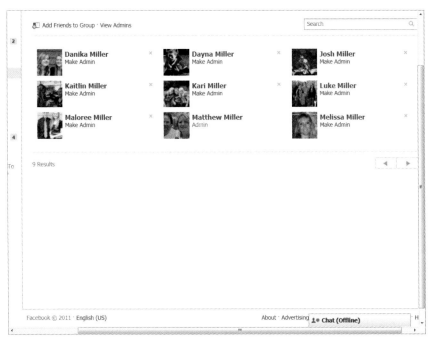

FIGURE 11-3 Group members and admin selection

You can choose from three privacy settings when you create your new group. If you don't choose one, Facebook chooses Closed as the default.

✛ **Open:** Anyone can see the group, who is in the group, and what members post. They cannot post to the group though because you have to be a member to do so.

✛ **Closed:** Anyone can see the group and who is in it, but all posts are only visible to members.

✛ **Secret:** Only members can see the group, who is in it, and what group members post.

I prefer the Secret Group setting because one of the main benefits of setting up a Group is having a private place on Facebook to share information and discuss issues with family and friends.

Join a Group

If you see a group in your search results that you would like to join, you can request to join the group by following these steps:

1. Find a group you are interested in and visit its page.

2. In the upper-right side of the group page, find the Join button and click it.

3. A confirmation pop-up appears after clicking Join. Your request to join the group will be sent to the Group admin.

HOW MANY GROUPS CAN I JOIN? You are limited to 300 Groups. If you reach that limit, you need to leave some to join new ones. If you request to join a group through this manner, a group admin must first approve your request before you become an official member.

WHY CAN'T I FIND A GROUP I KNOW EXISTS? Groups that are set up as secret groups do not appear in search results; therefore you cannot request to join these groups. You can only join them if a member gives you access.

You can also add a friend to a Group you are a member of after it is already up and running. If you want to do so, follow these steps:

1. Visit the Group page of a specific group to which you are a member.

2. Over in the left column under the Group name and Group profile picture, find the hyperlink labeled Invite People to Join and click it.

3. From the friend selector page, click your friends you want to invite (see Figure 11-4). You can also use the search box to find them faster.

4. Enter any email addresses to invite friends who are not yet on Facebook. To interact with the Group, they need to join Facebook, but will be given that opportunity after you invite them.

5. Add a personal message to your invitation.

6. Click the Send Invitations button to send out your Group invites.

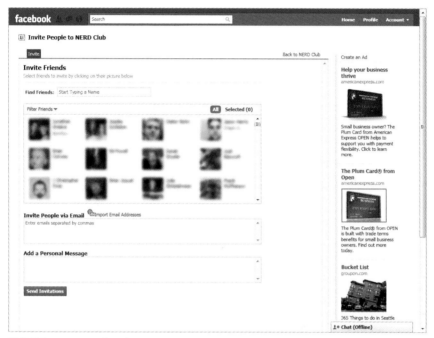

FIGURE 11-4 Invite friends to a group

After your friend receives the invite, through notifications, she can choose to confirm joining the group and will then become a member.

OLD GROUPS CAN'T ACCESS NEW GROUP FUNCTIONS You may find that some of the options detailed in this chapter are not available to you and your Group. Facebook launched a new Groups module in October 2010 (`http://blog.facebook.com/blog.php?post=434700832130`) and thus Groups created before then are still accessible to you, but they do not have access to many of the functions that newer groups do. The only way to combat this is to leave or delete your old group and create a new one in its place.

Leave or Delete a Group

You may have been a bit ambitious when you saw the Group functionality and joined more groups than you can manage. You may decide it is time to leave a Group because you are not getting much out of it. Or you may find that the Group you created is no longer valuable and want to delete it. The following steps describe how to perform these functions.

To leave a group, follow these steps:

1. Visit the specific page of the Group you want to leave.

2. Scroll to the bottom of the left column and you see the hyperlink labeled Leave Group. Click it.

3. A pop-up confirmation box appears. If you do indeed want to leave the group, click the Remove button.

After you leave the Group, you no longer receive Group notifications or get Group posts in your News Feed.

FACEBOOK AUTOMATICALLY DELETES GROUPS WHEN THEY HAVE NO MEMBERS   If you are the creator or first admin for the Group, you can go to the Group page and remove all the members of the group and yourself so that the Group has no members. The Group will then be removed from Facebook.

Share Content with a Group

After you join or start a Group, you need to share content and interact with Group members. The functionality used in other parts of Facebook is generally the same within Groups, with a few enhanced share options in Group chat, Group Events, and Docs, explained next.

POST A COMMENT

The key to posting content and interacting within a Group is to first always go to the Group page. The easiest way to navigate there is to look in the left column of your homepage and click the Group you want to access. Depending on the number of groups you are a part of, you may have to click See All to view all your groups.

When you are on a Group page, simply view the center column like you would on your Facebook page or that of one of your Facebook friends. To post a comment to the Group, follow these steps:

1. In the center column, make sure that the Post tab is active; if not click Post.

2. Click the text box with the grayed out words Write Something, and enter in the text of your post.

3. Click the Share button to post your comment.

After you post a comment that comment appears on the Group Wall and Group members can Like or comment on it like they would with posts you make on your own Wall.

POSTING COMMENTS VIA EMAIL The Group admin can also set up a Group email address (`mygroup@groups.facebook.com`) so that you can post updates to the Group via email if you do not have access to Facebook and want to use your email client to interact with the Group. The Group name does not need to match the email address, but it's usually a good idea to do so. To send an update via email, compose a new message to this email address in your preferred email program and then send it. The contents of your email body will appear as an update on the Group Wall, but anything you enter in the subject line will not appear.

SHARE A PHOTO, VIDEO, OR LINK WITH YOUR GROUP

Sharing photos and videos works just the way it does on your own Wall, only in Groups, just members (assuming it is a closed or secret group) can view the content.

To share a photo or video, simply click one of these options in the center column of your Group page and perform the same steps described in detail in Chapter 6 (How Do I Share Photos and Videos?).

To share a link to a website with your Group, simply click on the Link option in the center column of your Group page and perform the same steps described in detail in Chapter 3 (How Do I Navigate Facebook?).

CREATE A GROUP EVENT

One function that is unique for Groups is the ability to quickly create a Group event where all members of the Group are automatically invited. This saves more time than creating events through your standard Friends Selector. If you are a member of pre-October 2010 Group, then you likely will not have the option to create an event or it will be available to you as a link titled "Create Related Event" below the group picture. This option is only available for old groups that have fewer than 5,000 members.

To create an event within your Group, follow these steps:

1. Visit the Group page and click Event in the center column. The upper part of the center column changes to an Event entry form, as shown in Figure 11-5.

FIGURE 11-5 Creating a Group event

2. Enter a description for the event and fill out the remaining fields in the entry form.

3. Click Share to post the event and send out invitations.

DON'T FORGET YOU CAN ADD DETAILS Similar to the way you created an event in Chapter 7 (What Are Events and How Can I Use Them?), you can add more details and specify invitation settings by clicking the Add Details hyperlink. The details entry page, as shown in Figure 11-6, is where you can add details such as the event picture, end time, control invitation settings, and more.

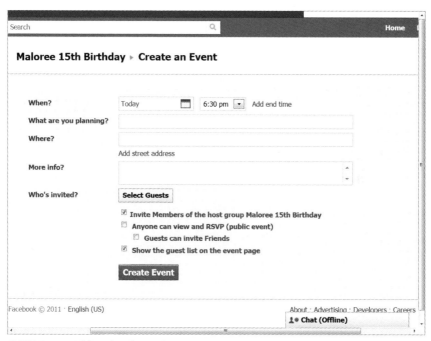

FIGURE 11-6 Adding details to a Group event

GROUP CHAT

One of the coolest features of Groups is the Group Chat functionality that enables you to chat online with multiple people in the same conversation. Chapter 5 (How Do I Communicate With Friends?) discusses Facebook Chat in detail and Group Chat takes that same experience and applies it to your entire Group so you can carry on conversations with all your family at one time.

To carry out a Group chat session, follow these steps:

1. Visit the page for the Group with which you want to chat.

2. In the upper-right column, you see the option to either Go Online to Chat (if you are currently offline) or Chat with Group (if you are online). Click one of these options to initiate a Group chat session.

3. A Group chat window opens in the bottom right of your page, and you can carry out a chat session just like what was detailed in Chapter 5 (see Figure 11-7).

FIGURE 11-7 Group chat session

WHY ISN'T GROUP CHAT AN OPTION FOR MY GROUP? Facebook has a limitation so that groups with more than 250 members do not have access to Group Chat.

As different people chat in the group, their profile picture appears to the left of their chat comment, so you can keep track of who is communicating.

GROUP DOCS

Group docs is a function that enables you to collaboratively create, write, and edit a basic text document. These documents can be edited and viewed by all members of the group and any member can add or remove sections of the document. It performs much like a wiki does and can be useful for things such as major event invitation creation, study group notes, proposal review and editing, and much more.

To create a document for your Group, follow these steps:

1. Visit the page for the Group you want to collaborate with and look in the center column for the word Doc link to the right of Share.

2. Click the Doc hyperlink and a document creation form appears, as shown in Figure 11-8.

3. Enter a title for the doc.

4. Enter text into the document. Basic editing tools for bold, italic, bulleted, and numbered lists are present.

5. Click Save to save and publish the document to the Group.

The text of the doc then appears in the Group feed. The doc appears with a solid gray bar to the left of doc text, which is different than a standard post.

WHERE CAN I FIND ALL GROUP DOCS? You can find your list of most recent docs in the right column of your Group page. Click the See All hyperlink to view all documents associated with your Group.

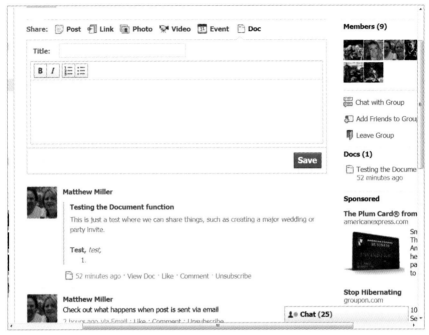

FIGURE 11-8 Initial document creation form

Now that a doc is present, follow these steps to view and edit the doc.

1. Find a doc on your Group page and either click the View Doc hyperlink at the bottom of the doc post or click on the document title found over in the right column.

2. Click the Edit hyperlink in the upper right of the doc view page.

3. Put your cursor into the doc, and edit the text as you want, shown in Figure 11-9.

4. Click the Save button to save the edited doc.

You also have the option to comment or Like the doc just like any other Wall post.

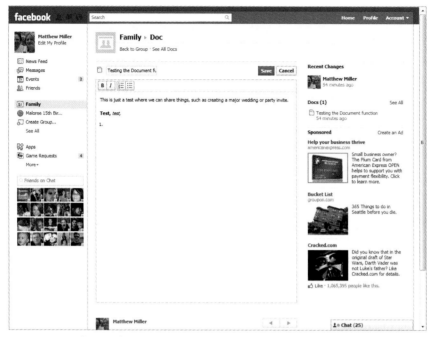

FIGURE 11-9 Editing a doc

GROUP NOTIFICATIONS

Email notifications for the Group can be managed by the admin but are also accessible to each member of the Group to manage for themselves. To access these settings, simply click on the Edit Settings button in the top right of your Group page. Therefore, each member of the Group can have different notification settings if they want to change them from what the Group admin assigned by default.

Available options for email notifications from your Group include the following:

+ When a member posts or comments

+ When a member posts

+ When a friend posts

+ Only posts I am subscribed to

Additionally, you can turn off all group notifications sent to your email and toggle the option to have group chat messages sent to you as well.

Related Questions

+ How can I add friends to create my Group? **PAGE 47**
+ Can I add events to my calendar? **PAGE 93**
+ Can I access Groups from my smartphone? **PAGE 132**

CHAPTER TWELVE

WHAT ARE FACEBOOK APPLICATIONS AND HOW CAN I USE THEM?

Although Facebook is primarily designed as a social network to facilitate communication with others, it is also an Internet platform accessible to developers. It is likely that your Facebook friends have invited you to play *FarmVille*, *Mafia Wars*, or some other game at some time; these are called Facebook applications. Other functions in Facebook, such as Events and Photos, are also considered applications; although they are better integrated into the Facebook experience. Applications are meant to enhance the social network experience and are available for games, utilities, sports, entertainment, and more.

What Is an Application on Facebook?

Applications are extra features connected through Facebook that enable users to perform more functions that enhance the user experience and take advantage of the social networking capabilities of the Facebook platform. Some of the applications integrated into your profile, such as Events and Photos, were made by Facebook developers and most people cannot even distinguish them from the Facebook site itself. Most applications on Facebook are created by third-party developers though and are freely accessible via external websites, desktop apps, and mobile apps. Zynga, one of the earliest developers on Facebook, launched a game called *Farmville* that has taken off in popularity and become a crowd favorite. Another one of its titles, *CityVille*, has a reported 89.9 million active users playing on a monthly basis. That is almost 1 in 5 Facebook members playing the game. Applications are popular and fun way to get the most out of your Facebook experience.

Find Applications

You may already have some applications on your Facebook page that you aren't aware of; click the Apps hyperlink in the left column of your Facebook page to see your current list of apps, as shown in Figure 12-1.

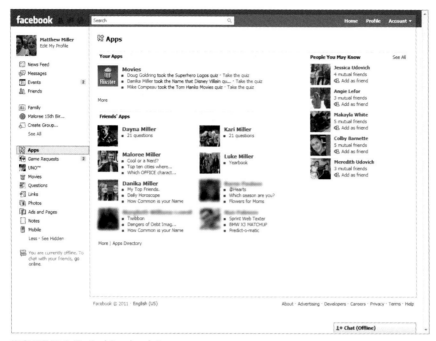

FIGURE 12-1 Typical Facebook Apps page

FIND APPLICATIONS IN THE APPLICATION DIRECTORY

If you don't have any applications yet, or you want to add more, the easiest way to find Facebook applications is to visit the Application Directory page at `www.facebook.com/apps/directory.php`, as shown in Figure 12-2. As you can see on this page, there are apps along the top that Facebook recommends, apps that Facebook thinks you may find useful in the middle section, and apps that your friends use in the bottom section.

You can see on the left that you can filter your application search using the following subject-based categories:

- Business
- Education
- Entertainment
- Friends & Family
- Games
- Just For Fun
- Lifestyle
- Sports
- Utilities

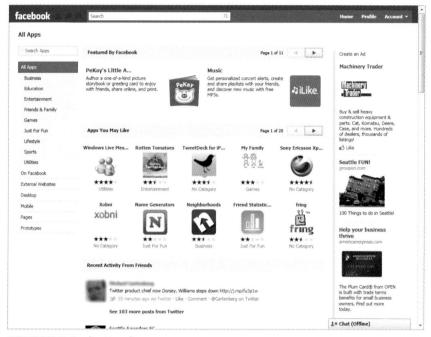

FIGURE 12-2 Application directory

Other selections on the left include the following platform-based categories:

+ All Apps
+ On Facebook
+ External Websites
+ Desktop
+ Mobile
+ Pages
+ Prototypes

Facebook states that the prototype applications are product experiments created by its engineers and can be buggy, as shown in Figure 12-3. Most of them are utilities that try to improve your Facebook experience; see Figure 12-4 for an example of a prototype application.

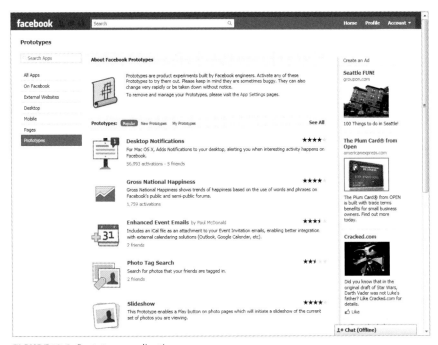

FIGURE 12-3 Prototype applications

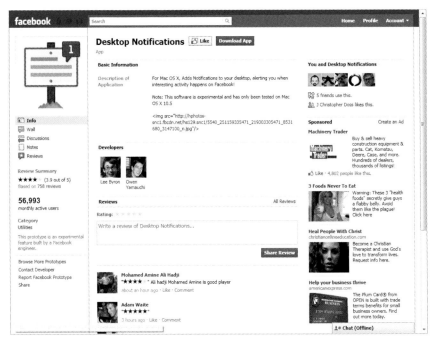

FIGURE 12-4 Typical prototype application

FIND APPLICATIONS YOUR FRIENDS LIKE

You can also find applications by looking in the left column of your Facebook home page and viewing the Applications and Games Dashboard that shows the latest games and applications that you and your friends have used, as shown in Figure 12-5. This is one way to discover what your friends like to play and what they recommend.

Your friends may also send you game requests or gifts from applications on Facebook you may want to try. You have the option to accept or reject these requests, which is discussed in more detail later in this chapter.

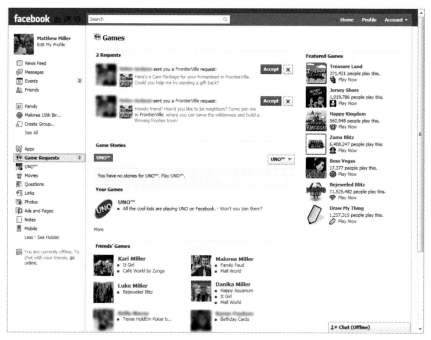

FIGURE 12-5 Games and Apps Dashboard

FIND MULTIPLE APPLICATIONS FROM ONE DEVELOPER

It is common to find that developers create more than a single application; therefore by looking at one application's page, you can often discover more apps from that same developer. The application page has reviews, discussions, events, and more to enable you to make an informed decision before adding it. See Figure 12-6.

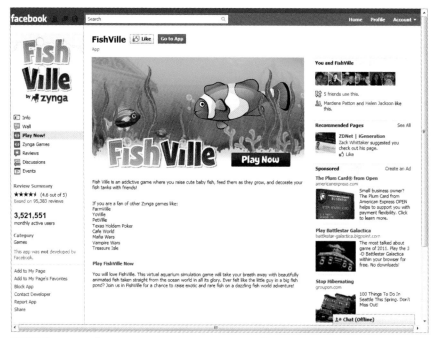

FIGURE 12-6 Application page suggesting more apps from one developer

Grant Applications Access to Your Information

When you find an application that you want to use on Facebook, you have to first grant access to that application. This entails allowing the application in question to access various parts of your Facebook profile information and use it to enhance the application experience. For example, some apps may post awards you earned to your wall while others may need your name to create a family history. Each application may ask to access different parts of your information, so make sure to check over the permission request, shown in Figure 12-7, before granting full access. Some of the most common areas that applications request access to include the following:

- Name
- Profile Picture
- Gender
- User ID
- List of friends

FIGURE 12-7 Granting application permission

Before you grant the application access to your information, you should check out the application to make sure it is safe to grant it access. To learn more about an application, follow these steps:

1. In the global Facebook search box, enter the name of the application you are considering.

2. Do NOT click the name of the application/icon that appears directly under your search result with the heading of Games or Apps. Look further down in the list under the Pages section and click the Application's page. You may need to select to see more results to gain access to the

Page information. You can also use the left-column filter to show only application pages.

3. After you find the application page (refer back to Figure 12-6 for an example), look at the Info tab, Reviews tab, and other data on the application to find out if it is indeed an application that you want to use and has a developer that has a verifiable history. You may be able to make this determination by the number of applications, positive reviews, and researching the company or developer on the Internet.

YOU CAN BLOCK APPLICATIONS If there are applications that you want to block from ever receiving your information, you can follow the preceding steps to learn more about an application and then in the left column of the application page scroll down and click Block App.

FACEBOOK MAKES IT CLEAR IF IT DID NOT DEVELOP THE APP Look in the left column of an app's page to see the Note from Facebook on whether the app was developed by Facebook engineers. Facebook makes this clear so that you know if you are granting access to your information to a third-party entity by stating, "This app was not developed by Facebook."

Use Applications

After you find an application and complete the authorization for the application requesting your information, you will be directed to the "canvas page" of the application (see Figure 12-8).

The canvas page is the launch page for the application. Here you can begin playing your game or utilizing the application for whatever is was meant.

FIGURE 12-8 Getting ready to play UNO

GAMES

The hottest selling category in software on nearly every platform (consoles, mobile, and PC) is games, and if you look at the most popular applications on Facebook, they too are games. Zynga has the most popular games with *CityVille, FarmVille,* and *Texas HoldEm Poker,* all with more than 37 million active users each.

Facebook games have different levels of interaction, but almost all of them are designed to take advantage of the social networking aspects of the plat-form in one way or another. Some games are played individually, and then the social part of it is applied as scores are compared and tallied. As you can see in Figure 12-9, Zuma is an individual game with the capability to quickly compare your score to your friends.

FIGURE 12-9 Playing Zuma on Facebook

One of my favorite games is Scrabble, which is set up for people to play virtually with one another without having to be online at the same time. You can play a turn and then return several days later to take your next turn while receiving notifications in the meantime as other players finish up their turn. Other games are even more interactive and enable share functions such as the following:

+ Share earned coins with friends. Coins, cash, and other rewards are collected or earned and banked so they can later be used to buy virtual goods, properties, etc. in the game.

+ Request virtual favors from friends for things like obtaining permits.

+ Invite friends to play and even join Facebook.

+ Visit your friend's virtual world and help them build things.

UTILITIES AND OTHER APPS

Utilities are applications that serve as tools to help you complete a task. You will find available utilities on Facebook in the Application Directory as mentioned earlier in this chapter. Integrated apps such as Photos and Videos are considered utilities in Facebook, and are discussed in detail in Chapter 6 (How Do I Share Photos and Videos?). Other popular utilities in Facebook follow:

- Windows Live Messenger
- Family Tree
- Birthday Calendar
- Notes (developed by Facebook engineers)
- Poll
- Twitter

Other applications include business apps and entertainment apps. Business apps are similar to utilities but focus more on handling transactions, helping you shop, and presenting deals and reward offers. Some popular business apps in Facebook follow:

- Bing
- Marketplace
- Contests
- Sweepstakes
- Shopping Mall
- Starbucks Jobs

You will also find an Entertainment category of apps in the Application Directory with apps that are focused on things such as music, movies, books, and other types of content related primarily to media experiences.

Spend Money on Facebook with Games and Apps

Facebook Credits are the virtual currency that you use to buy virtual goods in games and apps, but they are purchased with real money through your credit card, PayPal, or mobile phone wireless carrier. Many games let you play them for free, but if you want to build up your virtual world, then Facebook Credits can be used to purchase virtual goods.

To access Facebook Credits, follow these steps:

1. Click Account in the upper-right area of your Facebook page.

2. Click Account Settings.

3. Click the Payments tab on the Account Settings page, as shown in Figure 12-10. You can view your Credits balance and purchase more (see Figure 12-11), view your Credits purchase history, view your payment methods, and check your preferred currency (if you need to change the local currency).

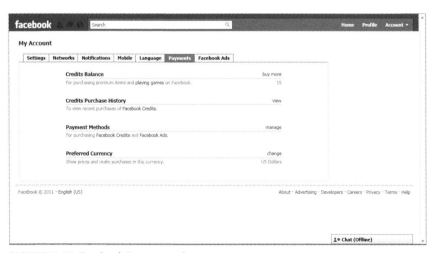

FIGURE 12-10 Facebook Payments tab

FIGURE 12-11 Purchasing Facebook Credits

HOW MUCH DO FACEBOOK CREDITS COST? The minimum amount to purchase is 50 Credits for $5. The more you purchase the larger discount you are given, so for $10 you can buy 105 Credits and for $100 you can get 1,120 Credits. Remember, this is real money.

You can also purchase credits from within the Games Dashboard or from within games directly. Make sure to check the Facebook Help section where it lists all the game titles where you can use your Facebook Credits.

Spending Money in Facebook Games

CityVille is currently one of the most popular games on Facebook, and as you can see in Figure 12-12, there are more than 90,000 reviews for the game. Figure 12-13 shows that you can pay real money via a credit card for virtual cash whereas Figure 12-14 shows that you can purchase game cards in retail stores and apply them to your game credit.

FIGURE 12-12 CityVille page with over 90,000 reviews

FIGURE 12-13 Buying virtual cash in CityVille

FIGURE 12-14 Redeeming game cards

Each game is a bit different in how they handle actual money in the virtual world; some have pre-priced packages such as CityVille while others allow you to purchase any amount of coins or goods you want. Many games that support purchasing coins or other types of credit have a store front that you can use to buy these tokens via credit card, as UNO does in Figure 12-15.

Remove or Delete Applications

You may eventually find that you want to remove or delete apps from your Facebook account. One of the quickest ways to remove an app is to go to the Apps and Games Dashboard in the left column and then follow these steps:

1. Find an app or game you want to remove and hover your cursor to the left of the app or game name. An X appears to the left of the name.

2. Click the X. A pop-up box appears (see Figure 12-16) with a few options to manage your notifications or to remove and block the app.

3. Click the red X to remove and block the app. Another confirmation pop-up appears.

4. Click the button to block the application so that the app can no longer get any information from you.

FIGURE 12-15 Buying coins for UNO

FIGURE 12-16 Managing your app from the Dashboard

You cannot find all your applications in the left-column dashboard however, because not all of them are used within the Facebook website. You may have mobile applications or applications that are integrated into other sites, so to access and manage these other applications, follow these steps:

1. Click Account in the upper-right area of your Facebook page.

2. Click Privacy Settings.

3. In the lower left of your privacy settings, find the words Apps and Websites; then click the Edit Your Settings hyperlink. Another page opens, as shown in Figure 12-17.

4. In the area labeled Apps You Use, click the Edit Settings button. A page listing all your authorized apps appears, as shown in Figure 12-18.

5. Click the X on the right to remove an app.

6. Click the Remove button in the pop-up confirmation box.

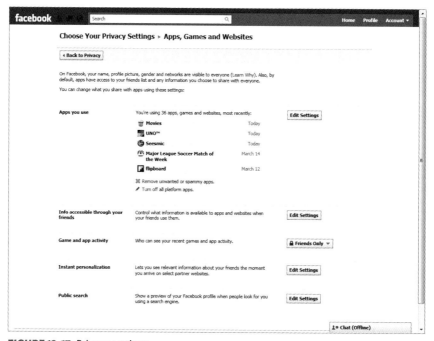

FIGURE 12-17 Privacy settings

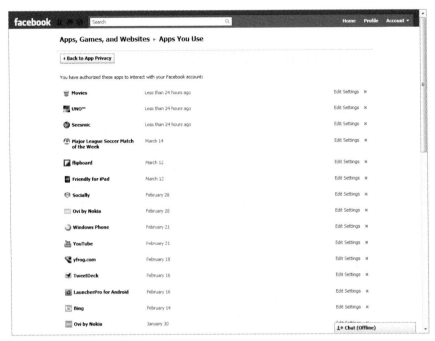

FIGURE 12-18 Managing apps you use

On this application settings page, all your authorized applications are listed, including those used from your mobile phones to access your Facebook account remotely.

Manage Application Settings

Every application is unique and also has unique settings. Previous sections discussed how to access application settings, but you can go back in and edit more specific settings for each of your applications. To manage application settings in Facebook, follow these steps:

1. Click Account in the upper-right area of your Facebook page.

2. Click Privacy Settings.

3. In the lower left of your privacy settings, find the words Apps and Websites; then click the Edit Your Settings hyperlink. Another page opens up.

4. In the area labeled Apps You Use, click the Edit Settings button. A page listing all your authorized apps appears.

5. Click the Edit Settings hyperlink to the right of your selected application.

6. Take the actions you want for the specific application, as shown in Figure 12-19. Settings for each application are different with varying degrees of available customizations. If you do not like the available settings, you can always choose to remove the application.

FIGURE 12-19 Manage settings for Seesmic

Related Questions

+ How can I add friends so I can play against them? **PAGE 44**
+ How can I use the Events application? **PAGE 95**
+ Can I use Facebook applications on my smartphone? **PAGE 128**

WHAT ARE FACEBOOK PAGES AND HOW CAN I SET THEM UP?

M ost of this book focuses on how to enjoy Facebook as an individual connecting with your family and friends; however, businesses, celebri-ties, bands, and different organizations also use Facebook to share informa-tion with users around the world. Official representatives typically manage these said Pages, but if you are starting your own business or are the resident Facebook expert for your company (and you will be once read this book) you can be the one who creates and administers Pages for your organization.

What Is a Facebook Page?

A Facebook Page (see Figure 13-1) is similar to a business website that you might find while browsing the Internet but is created and shared within the Facebook platform and includes support for extending the site with appli-cations and sharing functionality. The following types of entities create Facebook Pages:

+ Local business or place

+ Company, organization, or institution

+ Brand or product

+ Artist, band, or public figure

+ Entertainment (such as movies or books)

+ Cause or community

As you see, you can set up a Page for just about anything other than an individual or family pet. I have Facebook Pages for one of my websites and am an administrator for my company's Page.

WHY CHOOSE A PAGE INSTEAD OF A PERSONAL ACCOUNT? If you are an artist or have a brand to promote, Facebook optimizes the sharing experience if you set up a Page rather than a personal Facebook Profile page. These Pages include custom functionality for the different catego-ries so that a band Page, for instance, has a music player, video player, reviews, and more already provided simply by creating a new Page.

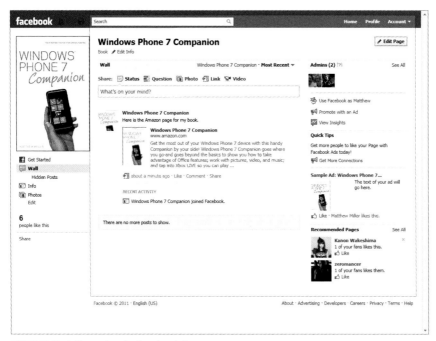

FIGURE 13-1 Example of a Facebook Page

Pages received updates in February of 2011, similar to the Profile UI update you find on your own Facebook page. These new features include the following capabilities:

+ Feature photos of your Page's most recent experiences at the top of your Page.

+ Highlight other Pages you connect with and the people who manage your Page.

+ Filter Page posts by Top Posts or Most Recent so that Pages look and function more like the general Facebook website individual users are used to.

Create a Page

Before you begin to create your organization's Facebook Page, you may want to browse around a bit so you can fully understand what a typical Page looks like and obtain ideas for creating a design before you jump in. Visit the

Discover Facebook Pages website (www.facebook.com/pages/browser.php) to browse some Pages that you are interested in (see Figure 13-2). You can click on the picture of the Page to Like it or click on the hyperlinked name of the Page to just view it.

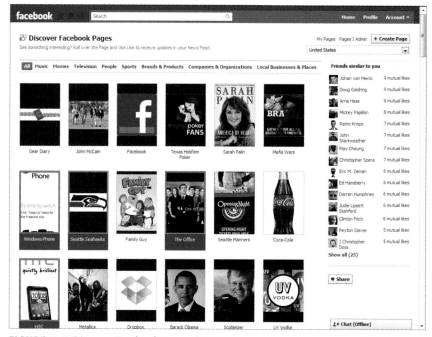

FIGURE 13-2 Discover Facebook Pages site

WHY SHOULD I LIKE A PAGE? When you Like a Page, a link to that Page appears on your personal Wall; thus choosing to Like a Page helps to promote it to your friends. Once you Like a Page, you can then see the Page's posts, receive updates, and more.

After you check out some Pages and have your own design in mind, follow these steps to create a new Page:

1. From the Facebook Pages discover page, click the Create Page button in the upper-right corner of your display. A new page with six large boxes appears.

2. Decide which category your organization fits into from the choices on this page, as shown in Figure 13-3.

3. Click one of the selections. A small form appears within one of the six boxes that you selected.

4. Fill out the form (they vary slightly based on the category you choose), as shown in Figure 13-4.

5. Click the hyperlink to read the Facebook Pages Terms and then click the box to agree to them.

6. Click the Get Started blue button to start creating your Page.

WHY CAN'T YOU FIND A PAGE FOR THIS BOOK? If you read the guidelines for Page names, any Page that has a variation of the word Facebook will be rejected; therefore I couldn't create a Facebook Page for this book, titled *Facebook Companion*. Ironic, isn't it?

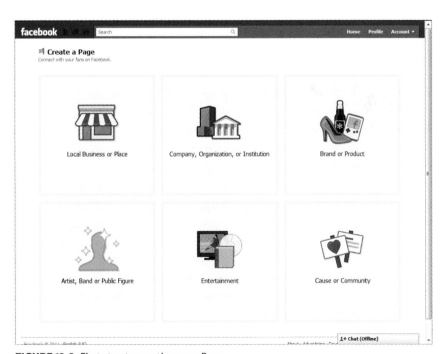

FIGURE 13-3 First step to creating your Page

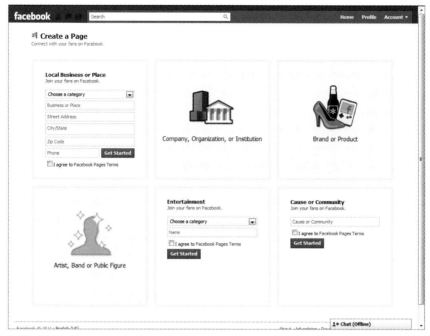

FIGURE 13-4 Forms for starting your Page

If you select an approved name and agree to the Terms, you see an unpopulated page appear with the name you selected at the top in the center (see Figure 13-5). This new page should appear much like your own individual Facebook page when you first set it up in Chapter 1 (Why Choose Facebook and How Do I Get Started?).

As you can see in the center column of your new Facebook Page, there are six areas for you to begin filling out:

+ Add an Image
+ Invite Your Friends
+ Tell Your Fans
+ Post Status Updates
+ Promote This Page on your Website
+ Set Up Your Mobile Phone

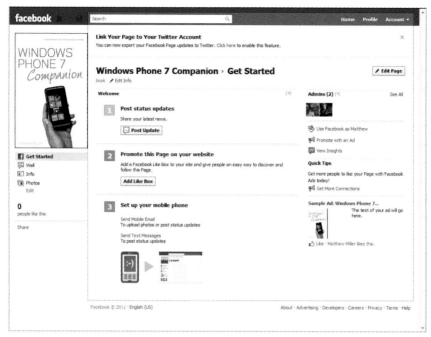

FIGURE 13-5 First view of your new Page

The image option is similar to your Profile picture, as discussed in Chapter 2 (How Do I Set Up My Profile?) but is for your organization or cause. You can invite your friends and tell your fans by using wizards that walk you through sending out notices or importing contacts in a few easy steps. You can connect to your mobile phone, enabling you to post status updates for your Facebook Page from a phone on the go, just like you learn to do in Chapter 9 (How Can I Use Facebook Effectively on My Mobile Phone?). You can also generate a Like box that you can then post on your website. For instance, if you're creating a Facebook Page for your book and you have a blog about the subject your book is on, you can put a Like icon on your blog that when clicked, enables the user to Like your Facebook Page. To create a Like box to post on an external website, follow these steps:

1. Click Get Started in the left column of your Page

2. Click on the Add Like Box button found as Item 2 in the center column. A page opens up describing the purpose of the Like Box and gives you options for customizing the box, as shown in Figure 13-6.

3. Fill out the custom info:

+ Facebook Page URL

+ Width of the box you are going to create

+ Color scheme

+ Toggles for faces, stream, and header

4. Click on the Get Code button.

5. Copy the HTML plugin code and paste it into your website's HTML code.

FIGURE 13-6 Creating a Like Box

In addition to these six primary areas, you can customize many more areas of your new Facebook Page before you start sharing your Page with folks. In the upper right of your new Page, click the Edit Page button; now look in the left column to find links to navigate to areas for the following:

+ **Your Settings:** Toggles are available for you to set up posting preferences and email notifications.

+ **Manage Permissions:** Page visibility, country restrictions, age restrictions, controls for who can post, blocklists, and profanity controls are all available for you to customize on this page. This is also where you can choose to permanently delete the Page if you ever decide to do so (see Figure 13-7).

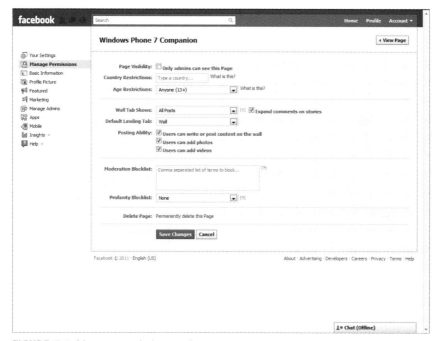

FIGURE 13-7 Manage permissions options

+ **Basic Information:** You can choose the category, create your Page username, and then add details that are customized for the type of page you created. For example, a book Page has fields for release date, genre, about, description, ISBN, publisher, awards, and website.

+ **Profile Picture:** This is where you can change the profile picture that you previously selected.

+ **Featured:** Pages that you Like from within your own Page, and other Page owners that you want to feature, are managed on this settings page.

✦ **Marketing:** This page simply gives you links to different ways you can promote your new Page, including advertising, telling your fans, getting a badge, and adding a Like Box.

✦ **Manage Admins:** You may want to have others help you manage and run your Facebook Page, and in this settings area you can set up other administrators. See the following section for more details on how to do this.

✦ **Apps:** Apps can be integrated into your Page, just like they can for your own individual Facebook account. By default, you can find apps for video, links, events, notes, and photos loaded into your new Page account. You can also click to browse and add more applications. Settings for each of the apps can be accessed from within this settings page.

✦ **Mobile:** This page simply presents the ways you can connect to your new Page with a mobile phone, but see Chapter 9 (How Can I Use Facebook Effectively on My Mobile Phone?) for all the specific details on how to connect with your mobile. You can also find the email address you need to upload photos and status updates via email to your Page.

✦ **Insights:** Clicking this link takes you to another full page that presents you with all your stats for your Page, including active users (daily, weekly, and monthly), interactions, and more. You can use this to target posts and figure out how best to market your organization's Page.

✦ **Help:** This simply takes you to the Facebook Pages help page on Facebook.

You can configure several available options to get your Facebook Page set up and working just how you want. Setup is quite easy because most areas have a wizard or are fairly self-explanatory when you start entering information.

Administer a Page

If you create a Page for an organization or cause, it is a good idea to have at least one other person available to help you; this person is known as an admin.

There is no limit to the number of admins you can set up for a Page, but each admin must be a Facebook member. To appoint other admins to your Page, follow these steps:

1. From within a Page that you administer, at the upper-right corner, click the Edit Page button. The available options detailed in the previous section appear in the left column.

2. Click the Manage Admins option.

3. In the text entry box, enter in an email address of a person that you want to add as an admin, as shown in Figure 13-8. You can also remove admins from this same page.

4. Click the Save Changes button to save any admin updates you make to your Page.

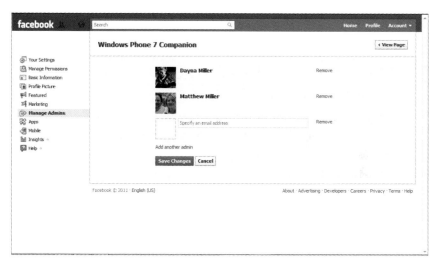

FIGURE 13-8 Appointing admins

AN EASIER WAY TO DESIGNATE ADMINS You can also click the People Like This link in the left column; then from the list of people who connect to your Page, click the Make Admin button to appoint them as an admin. See Figure 13-9.

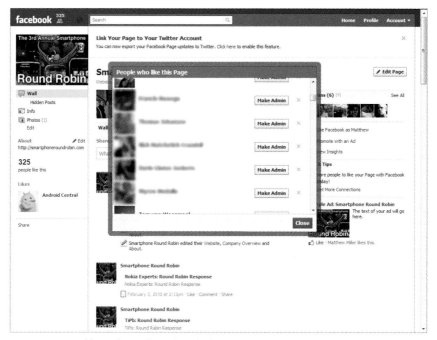

FIGURE 13-9 Adding admins from the Like list

After you set people up as admins, they can manage the Page from within their own Facebook account. To access one of the Pages that you administer, follow these steps:

1. From your own personal Facebook page, in the upper-right corner, find the word Account and click the drop down arrow.

2. Select the option to Use Facebook as Page. If you manage more than one Facebook Page a pop-up appears with the different pages as shown in Figure 13-10.

3. Select a Page to manage by clicking the Switch button to the right of the Page name. You then go to the Page and can see a view of the Wall.

4. To make any changes or updates to the Page, click the Edit Page button in the upper right and use the options in the left column to make any updates.

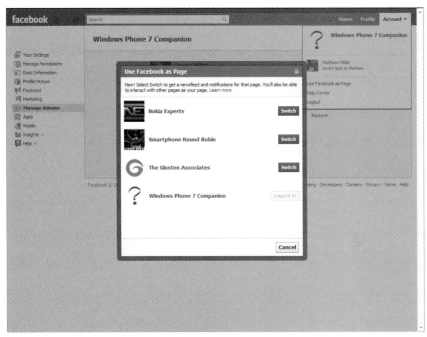

FIGURE 13-10 Select a Facebook Page that you administer

One of the duties of Page admins is to make sure that the Page complies with policies of the Page owner; for instance, if a follower is spamming the wall of your Page you may need to remove that user's connection to your Page or even permanently ban a follower. To remove someone connected to your Page, follow these steps:

1. In the left column of your Page, click the People Like This link under the number of people that Like your Page. This shows you all the people on Facebook who have chosen to Like your Page.

2. Click the X to the right of their name to remove them from your Page connection.

People can still later go back and Like your Page again after you remove them using this method however, so if they don't change their inappropriate behavior and you want to permanently ban a follower, follow these steps:

1. In the left column of your Page, click the People Like This link under the number of people that Like your Page.

2. Click the X to the right of their name.

3. Check the box next to Ban Permanently.

4. Click the Remove button.

Alternatively, you can also choose to ban people permanently by following these even simpler steps:

1. Hover your mouse cursor over the person who you want to ban, and click the Gear icon over to the right of the name.

2. Click the option to Remove Post and Ban User. A confirmation pop-up appears.

3. Click Remove Post and Ban User box to take the final action.

YOU CAN REMOVE POSTS FROM YOUR WALL You can also choose to remove posts directly from your Page's Wall, just like you can on your personal Facebook page. Doing so marks the post as spam, which will not be viewable to anyone except the user who posted the content and their friends.

Page Applications

Facebook includes some default applications when you create a Facebook Page so that you can provide a richer experience for your readers (see Figure 13-11). The following apps are provided on each new Page:

+ Photos

+ Video

+ Links

+ Events

+ Notes

+ Discussion Boards (only visible on Pages created where discussions are permitted)

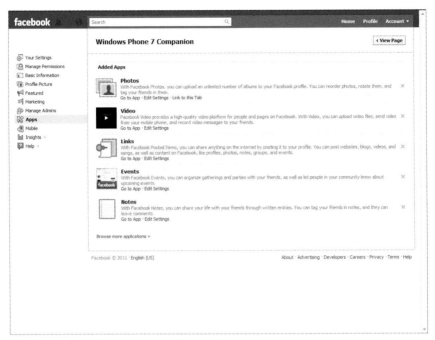

FIGURE 13-11 Applications provided for your Page

You can edit the settings in each of these apps by doing the following:

1. Go to the editor and select Apps from the left-column menu option.

2. Choose to add the app as a tab on your Facebook Page. After you enable the app, it appears in the center column of your Wall.

Promote Your Page

Now that you have a Facebook Page, you can share it with the world so that people visit it and discover your business, album, book, or cause. The fastest way to promote your Page is to have Facebook friends Like your Page so that it appears in News Feeds across the Facebook network. To help them find your Page to Like, post a link to your Page on your profile and on your friends' profiles. Simply follow the steps described in Chapter 3 (How Do I Navigate Facebook?) for sharing links.

After people discover your Page, it helps to keep fresh content on the Page through the following methods:

+ Regular Wall posts

+ Photo uploads

+ Video uploads

+ Page updates (described in the following section)

People who Like your Page receive these updates and continue to visit your Page.

CREATE AN UPDATE

A Page update is a way to inform people connected to your Page (through Liking it) that you have something new to share. You can choose to send updates to all your connections or even customize who receives these updates. To create an update for your Page, follow these steps:

1. From within a Page that you administer, look at the upper- right corner, and click the Edit Page button.

2. Click the Marketing option and choose to Send an Update. You are redirected to a page where you can create an update (see Figure 13-12).

3. Click and configure the audience who will receive the update.

4. Enter a subject for the update.

5. Enter a message to send to your followers. Attach a video, link, or other selected content to your update if you want.

6. Click the Send button to send out the update for your Page.

Updates appear both in the Other folder as a message in each user's inbox and as a notification. The update also appears on your Page Wall, so people can comment and Like the update from there.

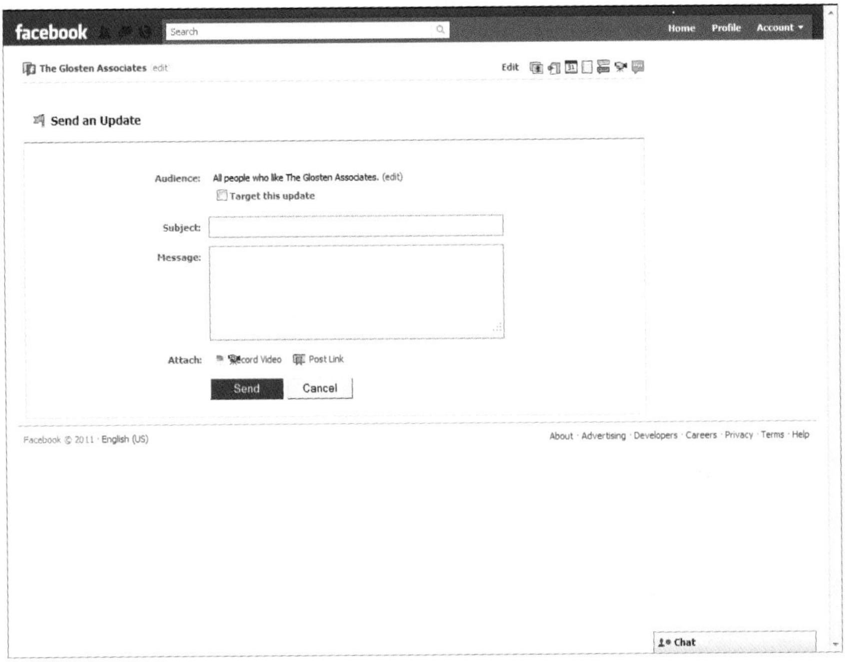

FIGURE 13-12 Preparing to send an update

Related Questions

+ How can I add friends to help promote my new Page? **PAGE 44**

+ Can I use Events to schedule an activity for my Page? **PAGE 95**

+ Can I use my smartphone to post Page updates? **PAGE 128**

CHAPTER FOURTEEN

HOW CAN I USE FACEBOOK TO BUILD AND PROMOTE MY BUSINESS?

In this chapter:

+   Using Facebook Ads For Your Business
+   Using Facebook as a Platform for Developers
+   Creating and Maintaining a Business Account

Facebook currently has more than 500 million active users and people spend more than 700 billion minutes per month on Facebook. To maintain this amount of users and use without implementing any required fees, Facebook needs to be funded in some way. These stats also reveal that Facebook has a captive audience for the savvy developer and entrepreneur for whom advertising and marketing can bring forth some serious results. Facebook offers several opportunities for those who want to advertise; providing a simple solution to reach millions of people.

Using Facebook Ads For Your Business

As discussed in Chapter 1 (Why Choose Facebook and How Do I Get Started?), Facebook is available to you for free to communicate and interact with other users, share photos and videos, chat with friends, play games, and much more. Although Facebook is available to you to use for free, the company incurs significant costs for servers, customer service, development, and more. Facebook Ads are one method to generate income to keep the social network free for end users.

FACEBOOK ADS TARGET SPECIFIC USERS

As detailed in Chapter 3 (How Do I Navigate Facebook?), you can find and leave feedback on Facebook Ads in the right column of your page, in apps, around photos, on Pages, and in other places sprinkled throughout the Facebook website. Facebook tries to present ads that are relevant and customized to you based on your viewing and browsing history. This can be mutually beneficial for users and advertisers: the user only sees ads that interest him, and the advertiser reaches more users who are likely to take interest in her product, service, or cause.

WILL FACEBOOK SELL MY INFORMATION TO ADVERTISERS? No. Facebook states that it will not sell your information and actively enforces policies to help protect your experience with third-party applications and ad networks.

ADVERTISING ON FACEBOOK

You may decide that you want to take advantage of these targeted ads and susceptible audience; if so, Facebook offers Facebook Ads for you to create and purchase from within your Facebook account. A great place to start is with Facebook's list of the top ten best practices for advertising on Facebook, which can be found at `www.facebook.com/ads/best_practices.php/` and includes:

+ Identify your advertising goals
+ Target your audience
+ Use keyword targeting to maximize return
+ Make your product stand out
+ Keep your ad simple
+ Use a strong call-to-action
+ Use an image
+ Direct people to a relevant landing page
+ Keep the user experience in mind
+ Evaluate your campaign performance

Once you've read these guidelines, you're ready to start creating your ad. To create a Facebook ad, follow these steps.

1. Look in the right column of your Facebook home page for the Sponsored area and click on the link to Create an Ad, as shown in Figure 14-1.

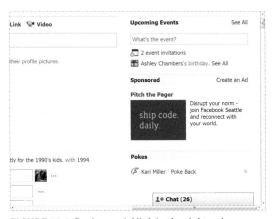

FIGURE 14-1 Design an Ad link in the right column

2. The Design Your Ad page opens with the following available entry fields, as shown in Figure 14-2:

✦ **Destination**: Select the type of page you want the Facebook ad to link to: either a Facebook Page you manage or a URL for an off network site.

✦ **Type, Story Type, and Destination Tab:** If you selected to post an ad linking to one of your Facebook Pages, fill these out accordingly.

✦ **URL**: Choose where a user's click will be sent (your business site) if you selected to enter a URL outside of Facebook.

✦ **Title**: Pick the title of your ad.

✦ **Body**: Enter text that appears on your ad.

✦ **Image**: Upload an image for your ad.

✦ **Preview**: See what it will look like.

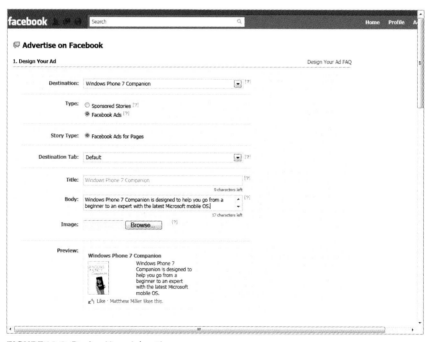

FIGURE 14-2 Design Your Ad options

3. After filling out these fields, click the Continue button to move to the next step, Targeting. In the Targeting step, you can find the following fields and selections, as shown in Figure 14-3:

✦ **Location:** Enter the location of the users you want to target. For example, if you are advertising for a single hair salon in Seattle, Washington, you'll want to limit your targeted audience to users whose location is Seattle.

✦ **Demographics:** Select the age and gender of your target audience.

✦ **Likes & Interests:** Type in common likes and interests your targeted audience will likely have; your choices will link to Facebook pages related to these likes and interests.

✦ **Connections on Facebook:** Filter through your existing connections to make the most of your Ad.

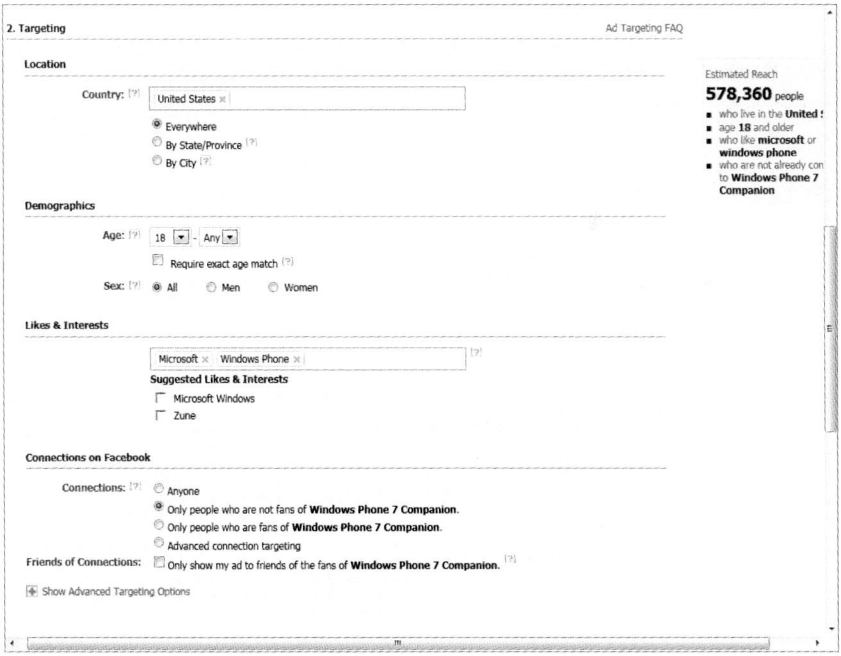

FIGURE 14-3 Targeting selection page

DON'T FORGET TO CHECK YOUR ESTIMATED REACH Notice in the right margin as you enter in targeting information that an estimated reach box appear with stats on your target audience (see Figure 14-4). As you change targeting parameters, your reach will adjust so you can figure out how to optimize your ad.

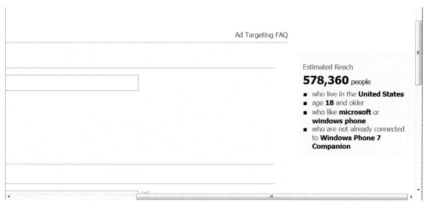

Ad Targeting FAQ

Estimated Reach

578,360 people

- who live in the **United States**
- age **18** and older
- who like **microsoft** or **windows phone**
- who are not already connected to **Windows Phone 7 Companion**

FIGURE 14-4 Real-time targeting estimates

You can also select from other advanced targeting options by clicking the link to Show Advanced Targeting Options, shown in Figure 14-5.

4. The next step in the process is to set up the campaigns, pricing, and scheduling plan for the ad. Click the continue button to reveal these available options, shown in Figure 14-6:

✦ **Account Currency:** Choose the type of currency you wish to use, such as U.S. dollars.

✦ **Account Time Zone:** Enter the time zone reflective of your ad.

✦ **Campaign & Budget:** Create a name and come up with a budget that you wish to designate at a per day or lifetime value.

✦ **Schedule:** Designate when your ad will run.

✦ **Pricing**: This is the estimated value that Facebook thinks you will pay for each click of your ad, based on your targeting options. You can also enter an advanced mode for setting a different bid on your ad than the one Facebook recommends.

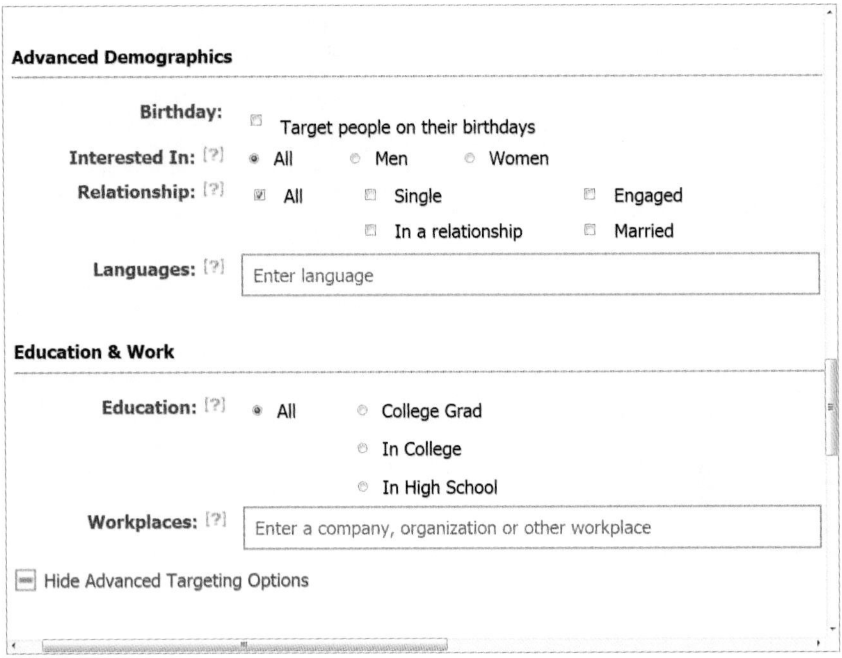

FIGURE 14-5 Advanced targeting options

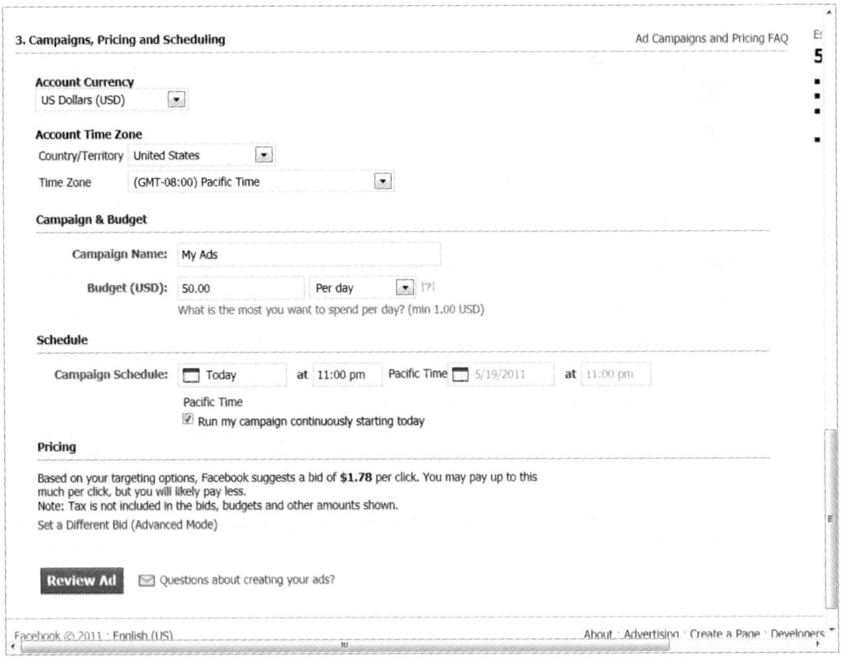

FIGURE 14-6 Campaigns, pricing, and scheduling

5. After filling out this section of your ad, click on the Review Ad button. You now see your ad available to review for accuracy (see Figure 14-7). Make sure to read the Facebook Statement of Rights and Responsibilities and the Facebook Advertising Guidelines, both linked on the Review Ad page, prior to finalizing and placing the order for your ad. If you are satisfied with everything, click the Place Order button to submit your ad to Facebook. You can pay for your ad with a credit card or through PayPal. If you see something wrong, click the Edit Ad button to make any necessary changes.

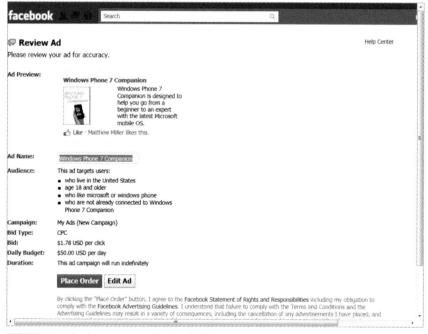

FIGURE 14-7 Review your new Facebook Ad

Using Facebook as a Platform for Developers

If your business is developing applications, the Facebook Platform offers many opportunities for developers to create applications for millions to enjoy. Facebook has detailed Getting Started guides to help those interested in developing for Facebook. Facebook has a new Graph application programming interface (API) and social plugins. Only basic programming skills are needed to design for on its platform. It is free to build on the Facebook Platform, and you gain access to its APIs and social plugins, and get help with building a mobile application. You can also choose to hire a programmer using the Developer Forum.

If you design your game or application with the Facebook Credits API and it supports payment of virtual goods via the Facebook Credits system then you receive 70 percent of the revenue from these virtual goods transactions. When you sign up to be a developer you enter in your financial institution information and Facebook pays you twice per month. There are various reports you can run within your developer account to track payments.

SOME STATS ON USING FACEBOOK CREDITS Facebook provides data noting that more than 350 apps and games currently use Facebook Credits and 22 of the top 25 games are included in this figure. There are also more than 150 developers using Facebook Credits.

Starting in July of 2011 Facebook requires all social game developers to process payments through Facebook Credits. Facebook states there are three primary benefits to using the Facebook Credits system for app purchases.

- ➕ **Increase your revenue:** Facebook sees higher conversion rates and increased average revenue per user when the payment system is integrated and easy. Millions of users also have their Facebook Credits information stored on the site so it is easier for them to pay for items.

- ➕ **Reduce costs:** You do not need to build and localize payment options, you get instant access to multiple payment methods (gift cards, direct debit, special offers), and you will reduce your fraud and customer support costs by letting Facebook handle all of that through their system.

- ➕ **Grow your business:** Facebook offers special incentives to get featured placement on the games dashboard and premium ad targeting. You also get access to test new beta products and get advice from Facebook teams.

Creating and Maintaining a Business Account

As detailed in Chapter 13 (What Are Facebook Pages and How Can I Set Them Up?), you can create Pages for your business after you have a personal Facebook account and then simply select to manage that Page from within your personal account login. Some people, however, may want to use Facebook only to administer Pages and Facebook Ads, and as a result, Facebook created the option for business accounts.

With a business account, you have the ability to do the following:

+ Administer the account directly from the business with no individual Facebook account association.

+ View and edit Pages and Ads created with the account.

+ Add Page content such as photos, videos, and events.

+ View statistics related to Pages and Ads.

You cannot, however, perform the following functions with a business account:

+ View the profiles of users on the site or other content that does not live on the Pages you administer.

+ Appear in a search.

+ Send or receive friend requests.

Business accounts are meant for just that: a business. They are typically monitored by a social media expert and they are not connected or linked to an individual account. Similar to a company credit card used only for company purchases, Facebook business pages are used only for business purposes, explaining their limited capabilities.

To create a business account, you first need to create a Facebook Ad or Facebook Page, without having an individual account. To do so, follow these steps:

1. Go to www.facebook.com (make sure you are logged out of your individual account if you have one).

2. Bypass the Sign Up form and either click the button to Create a Page below the form or look to the bottom navigation bar and click the link to Advertising.

3. From here, follow the steps listed in the previous section or in Chapter 13 (What Are Facebook Pages and How Can I Set Them Up?). Just be sure to choose, "Local Business or Company" in step 2.

CAN I HAVE AN INDIVIDUAL ACCOUNT AND A BUSINESS ACCOUNT? No. Facebook does not allow multiple accounts and treats this as a serious violation of its Terms of Use, so make sure whoever sets up the business account does not have an individual Facebook account, or if he does, that he deleted the account first.

Related Questions

✦ Where will my ads be placed on the site?   **PAGE 35**

✦ What kind of applications can I develop for Facebook?   **PAGE 180**

✦ How can I create a Page to also promote my business?   **PAGE 201**

✛ INDEX